Honeymoons in Style

Dr. Jill Nash and Carlo Nash

LUXURY BACKPACKERS

Footprints on Phillippine beach.

Honeymoons in Style

Palace in Tokyo.

Amanpulo Beach

Introduction

The term honeymoon has been traditionally recognized as a holiday taken by newlyweds to celebrate their marriage in intimacy and seclusion. Couples often use the opportunity of a honeymoon to take a trip of a lifetime – providing memories for the future as well as a chance to splash out before settling down to the responsibilities and realities of married life.

We embarked on our own honeymoon a year ago, and we couldn't understand why for such an important (and indeed expensive) event in any couples life, there were very few books on the subject. Of course, there are plenty of nice hotel books and numerous resort catalogues 'selling' honeymoons, but none that were 100% impartial and independently written - and certainly none that incorporated different styles of adventures together with unusual destinations.

As with most couples we enjoy a variety, so our honeymoon was a complete mixture of culture, action, gastronomy and relaxation – but it took us nearly 10 months to plan and research (almost the same time as planning the actual wedding!).

This inspired us to write 'Honeymoons in style', we wanted to share with you some of the personal travel experiences, destinations and adventures that we think are perfect for any style of honeymoon. Whether you seek action, beach or culture – whether you only have a long weekend or 6 months we are sure you will find something in our book to suit you.

This is the second book in our series of 'Adventures in Style' and in-keeping with the 'Luxury Backpackers' brand we hope to inspire you with our independently written experiences that break away from the clichéd honeymoon, while equally offering an opportunity to enjoy those first precious moments together as a newly married couple.

Congratulations on your wedding, we hope you enjoy every moment of your honeymoon (and future life) together.

Jill & Carlo

Key to Places to Stay:

= Under £150

= Under £250

= Over £250

Before you start...
what kind of honeymoon
would you like?

Action

Beach

Gastronomy

Spa

City

Culture + Art

Preface

Memorable honeymoons are all about creating a heady travel experience for two. And what could be more sexy and inspiring than 'luxploring' – the perfect combination of adventures by day, sheer indulgence by night. As travel has become the pastime of the masses, and couples are marrying later in life, chances are you're well versed globetrotters. Two weeks on the beach in a five-star resort just doesn't deliver the holiday of a lifetime anymore. The solution is right here in Jill & Carlo Nash's inspiring book which implores you listen to your adventurous, independent side and combine it with the most decadent accommodation out there.

As travel editor of You & Your Wedding magazine, I've been on hundreds of 'honeymoons' and by far the most memorable have combined drop-jaw beautiful resorts with wild adventure. Discovering the frenzy of Marrakech just when the riad craze was kicking off, hiring an old Citroen 2CV and driving through the lower Atlas Mountains and discovering the hippy coastal hangout of Essouira remains a romantic revelation. You don't have to go far off the well-trodden honeymoon trail, you just have to do things your way.

Indonesia is a great source of luxploring. Bali may be a honeymoon cliché, but go slightly off the beaten track and you'll still find ridiculous indulgence and adventure. Amankila near the verdant coastline of East Bali is hard to beat surrounded by ancient villages and stunning scenery. Indonesia has over 17,000 islands, so why not fly a bit further east to the much less visited island of Sumba where the lush forests and ancient tribal culture lie waiting, not to mention surfing, diving, mountain biking, horse-riding and trekking. Nihiwatu, an exclusive eco-luxe hideaway with just 10 luxurious thatched bungalows is the stuff of dreams. Heady indeed.

Jane Anderson
Travel Editor
You & Your Wedding

Top. Moroccan Spices.
Bottom. Marrakesh medina.

Top 3 honeymoon tips

1. Let your luxury hotel spoil you rotten. Tell them you're honeymooning and your VIP rating should rocket with romantic dinners on the beach, petal strewn candlelit baths for two and champagne on ice.

2. Venture outside your comfort zone and bend to your new spouse's desires. If she likes scuba diving, give it a go, if he likes climbing a volcano to see the sunrise, give it a whirl. Compromise and bonding makes a great start to married life.

3. After a hard day's adventure, book a sexy spa session for two. Most luxury resorts have couples suites in the most beautiful settings. I'll never forget watching my naked partner being showered down after a Lulur scrub by a delicate Balinese therapist who then guided him to a flower-filled bath where I was similarly pampered and waiting!

View of the Eiffel Tower over the River Seine.

FRANCE

Paris | Corsica | Cote d’azur + Province | Reims

FRANCE

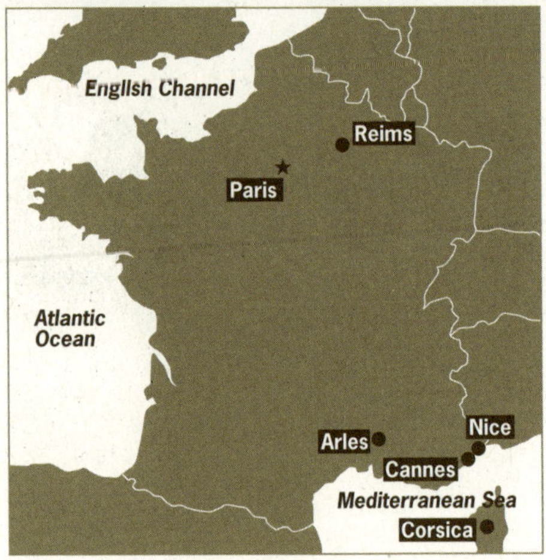

Why is this place so special?

France is synonymous with everything chic, seductive and stylish. Whether it's champagne, perfume, fashion or cheese (a French obsession) the French seem to do it with flair, grace and perfection. It is no wonder that the French are a fiercely proud nation and rightly so. France is tremendously endowed with art galleries, rich history, dramatic landscapes, hidden beaches and chic boutiques, not to mention superb gastronomic delights with varieties from every region.

The French are complete perfectionists when it comes to food. The combination of quality local produce, regional styles and lavish cuisine together with the ambiance, make up the age-old love affair with food. Today, gastronomic excellence is rewarded around the world with Michelin stars (3 being the highest), which were introduced in 1926 and although the French and Italians may argue amongst themselves who claimed to invent 'haute cuisine', undoubtedly France has developed its own rich culinary traditions - so whether you choose to eat in a Michelin star restaurant or buy some local produce from a bustling street market for a picnic, you won't be disappointed with the superiority of the food.

As the largest country in Western Europe, France's scenery is both stunning and diverse, from the rolling hills of the vineyards to the sandy beaches of the South and rugged coastline of Corsica you'll be spoilt for choice. Although Paris has been celebrated for centuries for its stunning and symmetrical architecture and romantic joie de vivre and you'll see many locals strolling along the grand boulevards and picnicking in parks watching the world go by; there are many other beautiful and stunning cities and towns each with their own charm and character.

Top. Eiffel tower in the distance.
Bottom. Metro signage.

The modern architecture of the cities intersects more humble and earthy architecture of the rural towns and villages, which makes France especially alluring to romantics. French architecture throughout the more recent centuries, though unique and different in each individual structure, is characterized by both beauty and grandeur, as evidenced in such structures as the Château de Versailles, Paris's Notre Dame, Arc de Triomphe, and Eiffel Tower. The Louvre museum's newer pyramid structure is an example of the forward-moving direction of France's architecture and design, and the Château de Versailles is reminiscent of France's grand and opulent royal history.

France offers an unparalleled choice of world-class places to stay from medieval châteaux to city gems, rural farmhouses and cosy chalets. So whether you are an outdoor action hero, a gastronomic lover or a hopeless romantic there is enough choice to satisfy every type or honeymooner. And just a hop away from the UK means that France is very accessible for those who want a long weekend or who aren't keen on flying, but still want a stylish, memorable escape.

Fast Facts

Capital: Paris.

Location: Western Europe, bordering 6 European countries, Spain, Belgium, Italy, Germany, England, Switzerland, and surrounded by the Bay of Biscay, the English Channel and the Mediterranean Sea.

Population: 60,876,136.

Religion: Roman Catholic 88%, Protestant 2%, remainder Jewish and Muslim.

Languages: French 100%, rapidly declining regional dialects and languages (Provencal, Breton, Alsatian, Corsican, Catalan, Basque, Flemish).

Opposite page. From top. Creed perfumerie Paris, shopping at Louis Vuitton, Eiffel Tower at night.

Getting there and exploring around

There are major airports in most French cities, and smaller airports served by "low cost" carriers such as Flybe, Easyjet and Ryanair. The five biggest French airports are: Paris Charles de Gaulle, Paris Orly, Nice, Toulouse and Marseilles where British Airways, BMI and Air France fly directly from the UK. You can sail or drive to France from Dover, Newhaven, Portsmouth, Poole and Weymouth, popular companies are P&O ferries, Seafrance, LD Lines and Brittany Ferries. The most convenient and increasingly popular way of travelling to France is by train from London to Paris or Lille. The Eurostar is quick, convenient and for those wanting privacy and extra comfort, there are also first-class seats with meals, free newspapers and priority check-in.

Exploring around France there are several options, the direct TGV (fast speed train) connects from Paris and Lille to a large number of French towns and cities, including Bordeaux, Rennes, Nantes, Dijon, Besançon, Avignon, Aix en Provence, Marseilles, Montpellier, Perpignan or Nice. It is worth knowing that by changing at Lille (instead of Paris), you do not need to change stations or cross the city as Eurostars and French TGVs share the same platforms at Lille station. Book a first-class 'couchettes' cabin for some privacy and extra comfort.

Driving in Paris is a nightmare, so it's best to travel around using the efficient 'metro' or walk. If you're planning to use lots of public transport in Paris, the best solution is to take a visitor's pass, 'Paris Visite' these passes are available on a 1, 2, 3 or 5 day basis, and cover all types of official public transport in the central area or suburbs.

Cycling across France is also increasingly very popular, either by guided tour companies or self-guided. Delux Cycle Tours are an independently run cycle company offering tours around Loire Valley, Dordogne and Province region with châteaux and boutique style hotel accommodation – a good choice for those wanting a to enjoy the outdoor scenery and stay in stylish places.

Best time of year to visit

The best time to visit Paris is usually around May and June, as well as September. Temperatures are warm (but not too hot as it sometimes is in August), and you'll escape the summertime crowds that tend to arrive in July. If you don't mind the crowds, you'll see the 'Tour de France long –distance cycle race and Bastille Day held every July 14th where most towns and cities organize opulent firework displays and in Paris you'll see the military parade along the Champs Elysees.

The best time of year to visit Southern France and the French Riviera is late spring, summer, or early Autumn. The weather is sunny and warm - perfect for the beaches of Nice, Cannes and Antibes. The late Autumn and winter are typically cooler, and rain and wind can be plentiful. However, tourist crowds are non-existent during that time of year, so if you don't like the beach and don't mind the weather, it's not a bad time to visit.

The best time to visit Corsica is June. Average temperatures rise and the sea is warm. At this time of year Corsica is still relatively quiet, and there is nothing better than finding the beach all to yourself. June is also the perfect time for walking, or exploring the local sights.

? Must know before you go

Learn the lingo. Not just to impress your new husband or wife, but to make an effort and earn you some respect with the locals. Even if it is just 'S'il vous plait', 'Merci' or 'Bonjour' it'll take you five-minutes to master the basics.

Pharmacy in need. It's good to know that the pharmacists in France are able to prescribe basic medications and antibiotics.

Opening hours. If you're travelling through France, and want to stop and buy Fresh bread for a picnic, don't forget that many small shops close for up to two hours in the middle of the day. Boulangeries often stay open beyond the traditional midday closing hour, but after 12.30 you may well find a locked door if you stop off at a village bakery.

Highlights

Day trip to Versailles. Visit the romantic and opulent Château de Versailles, stroll around the gardens and take a picnic.

The art trail. Follow the footsteps of Van Gogh in Arles, buy fresh produce from the market town of Aix-en-Province and bathe on a sun-drenched private beach along the Cote d'Azur.

Rambling around. Hike around Corsica's dramatic mountains or drive the scenic West coast road from Ajaccio to Calvi.

Champagne tasting. Drink some of the world best champagne and stay in the bustling centre of Reims.

Tip for the Trip

"Inform your bank before you travel to ensure there won't be any difficulties using your card abroad. The unfamiliar spending patterns might cause them to suspect fraud and they may 'block' your card – leaving you stranded, frustrated and very embarrassed."

Carlo

Top left. Hall of Mirrors at the Château de Versailles. **Top right.** Louvre.

Adventure: City
Destination: Paris

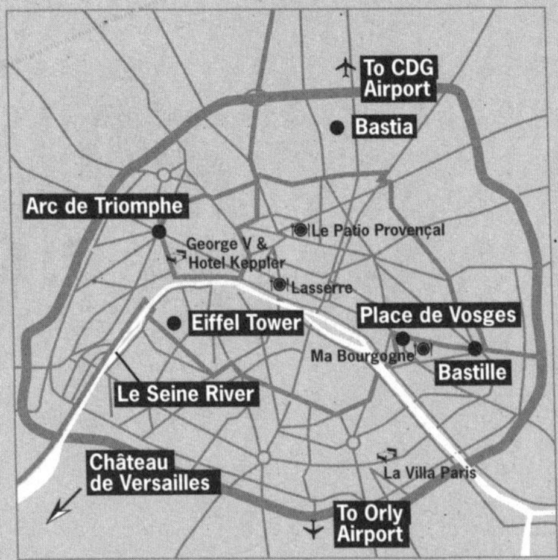

Regional Information

City style doesn't come any slicker than Paris. It's a perfect destination for hopeless romantics, shop-a-holics, art lovers and architectural buffs and with plenty of varied nightlife it's an excellent destination for those who also enjoy a spot of clubbing. You can easily visit Paris for a long weekend if you are short on time or spend a romantic 'first night' of your honeymoon here before exploring other parts of France. Just wandering around Paris unguided and on foot is a sheer delight, but if you are only here for a few days you might want to swot up on the highlights before your trip to save yourself time when you arrive.

The Parisian landmark 'Le Tour d'Eiffel' (Eiffel Tower) and one of the most recognized structures in the world is named after its designer, engineer Gustave Eiffel is still one of Paris's top attraction. Although very clichéd as an attraction and often over-crowded it is still a must-see for any couple, especially if it is your first time in Paris. Whether you decide to climb the 674 steps to the second level or take the lift to the summit or view its impressive strobe lights from a boat on the river 'La Seine' it's iconic and impressive. As with any of the attractions in Paris, it's best to arrive early or late to avoid the queues.

The 200-year-old Arc de Triomphe, is also one of France's most iconic monuments and the epicentre of city-planner Baron Haussmann's star of boulevards; it is certainly worth clambering up its many internal stairs to peer down the very symmetrical tree-lined Champs Elysées and enjoy pleasingly photogenic panoramic views of the entire city.

Although Paris is littered with art museums from the stunning Grand Palais to the sculptured Musee d'Orsay – there is no-where that has the sheer diversity and grandness of the Musee du Louvre. The stunning glass pyramid entrance (which featured notoriously in the Dan Brown film 'Da Vinci Code') is another one of Paris' top attractions.

The Louvre is a maze of art, featuring famous works such as Leonardo Da Vinci's Mona Lisa, The Virgin and Child with St. Anne, Madonna of the Rocks, Jacques Louis David's Oath of the Horatii, Delacroix's Liberty Leading the People and Alexandros of Antioch's Venus de Milo and you could easily spend a few days here just getting lost. You can visit the museum independently and pick up an audio guide (the museum have rolled out their own 50 minute tour of 'Da Vinci Code' narrated by actor Jean Reno) or you can opt for a full day 'Da Vinci Code' walk organised by many of the local tour operators. It is worth knowing that the fountains that line the area outside the central courtyard also make an excellent spot for bathing your feet, reading a book and watching the world go by.

Shopping is a serious Parisian pastime, and everywhere you look the French women (and men) are immaculately dressed. Rue du Faubourg Saint-Honoré is one of the city's famous long streets full of designer boutiques; a local favourite is La Collette, a celebrated lifestyle shop stocking an eclectic range of art, fashion, books and a café – it even has an ubercool water bar where you can sample one of the hundred varieties of water.

There are also plenty of independent boutique shops located in the Marais (4th quarter). This area is a hidden maze of antiques, art aswell as unkown fashion designers and the more celebrated French designers such as Barbara Bui. The Marais is renowned for being a very fashionable quarter for Sunday lunch, especially in the Place de Vosges where numerous artists gather and muscians play out a few tunes. Being predominantly the Jewish district – everything is open on Sundays, unlike the rest of Paris.

Adventure: City
Destination: Paris

Galeries Lafayette is as famous as the Eiffel Tower for shop-a-holics, its stunning dome shaped building filled with designer brands from food to clothing will awaken the shopper in anyone. This store isn't just for shoppers but also architectural lovers, the building is bursting with decadent details from the stone carvings to the stained glass and for those gasping for refreshments there is a champagne bar and complementary purified water on all levels. Printemps (also situated on Boulevard Haussmann) is also another French institution, the Paris store maybe slightly more commercial than Galeries Lafayette, but equally a destination in itself.

If you are tired of shopping you might find yourself in one of the many 'green parks'. 'Jardin du Luxembourg', is a favourite for Parisians, featuring chestnut groves and pretty terraces. If you happen to be visiting in the summer (July to August), parts of La Seine are transformed into beaches, where tons of sand are crated in, potted palm trees are placed and beach chairs and umbrellas are arranged. Great for topping up your tan, but don't expect to be bathing in the river.

Further a field, visit Versailles, which is one of Paris' most affluent and leafy suburbs and site of the very grand and famous Châteauxx de Versailles. Louis XIV (1643-1715) was France's longest-reigning most extravagant monarch. His grand palace at Versailles could accommodate 20,000 people in its 700 rooms. A tour of the Grand apartments in the palace is an absolute must; you can also take the little train around the gardens and fountains or paddle around the Grand Canal with a rowing boat. It is a day-trip from Paris (located only 23km away) and a popular retreat for locals and visitors alike, at weekends you'll see couples and families relaxing with pastry filled picnics and sipping local wine.

As night falls, Paris really comes alive and there are numerous places from chic rooftop bars to all-out nightclubs. Bar hopping in the Marais although very cool and stylish its not for everyone, renowned for being the 'gay quarter' and epicentre of the Jewish community it is also the centre of quirky bars and restaurants. Narrow lanes and buzzing cafes make it an excellent destination for those who don't like mainstream, commercial places. The Lizard lounge offers an underground cellar bar with DJ's belting out tunes till 2am. Those who want something more up-market then head to the 18th quarter where you'll find a hidden boutique hotel with an ice bar. Hotel Kube is very cool and hip among the young urbanites of Paris, and has the only ice-bar in France. Wrap up in furry hats and gloves and down very strong vodka in sub-zero temperatures. Book ahead for a 30-minute stint.

The VIP Room, formerly a cinema foyer, is easily one of Paris' most popular style bar. This club underwent a hugely expensive refurb - the interiors are glossy, dramatic and as futuristic as a sci-fi film set. The Panoramic Bar located on the 33rd floor of the Concorde La Fayette hotel, has splendid views of the Eiffel Tower and the Arc de Triomphe. Great for a more cosy romantic night whilst soaking up the impressive views of the city's skyline.

Below left. A superior suite at Hotel Keppler. **Below right.** Lasserre.

Stylish Places to Stay

Decadent: George V. Refined luxurious and decadent, George V is a Parisian treasure. The rooms are extravagant with luxurious Bulgari filled bathrooms and amazing views over the city. A spa offering a variety of treatments from pedicures to facials making you feel pampered and special. Highly recommend for the first night of a honeymoon.

Terrace chic: Hotel Keppler. Situated in the prestigious area of Paris (Champs-Elysées) and noted as the latest creation by celebrated designer Pierre-Yves Rochon, this 34 room mansion hotel is a perfect example of the very best in boutique hotel style. They have a cosy bar and elegant winter garden perfect for couples wanting intimacy and the top floor suites also have balconies overlooking the Eiffel Tower.

French home: La Villa Paris. A small intimate, but luxurious B&B and with only 4 rooms the service is warm, friendly and very personal. Located in the 13th quarter near Parc Montsouris, a French neighborhood with true French charm. This red brick 1920' s mansion is beautifully decorated and rates are very reasonable. You can even hire the whole place out if you want complete privacy.

Delicious Places to Eat

French haute cusine: Lasserre. Opulent, elegant with incredibly classic French food such as the classic foie gras or canard a l'orange located in the prestigious area of Franklin Roosevelt. Men must wear a jacket and tie. Prices are a little steep but the menu degustation is a seven-course delight.

Purely Province: Le Patio Provençal. Offering tasty traditional French food from the Province region. This highly regarded local delight is always packed, but worth the wait. Located in the 17th quarter and a walk away from metro 'Villiers'. Perfect for a long lunch and reasonable price.

Bistro Parisian: Ma Bourgogne. Located in Place de Vosages, where during the weekend many artists play music under the arcades surrounding the square, creating a great atmosphere. This traditional French kitchen with regional varieties from Burgundy and Central France, such as escargots de Bourgogne, saucisson from Beaujolais, and steak tartare are enjoyed on the terrace overlooking the gardens and square.

Right from top. Bonafacio, Corsica. Ile de Cavallo, Corsica.

Adventure: Action
Destination: Corsica

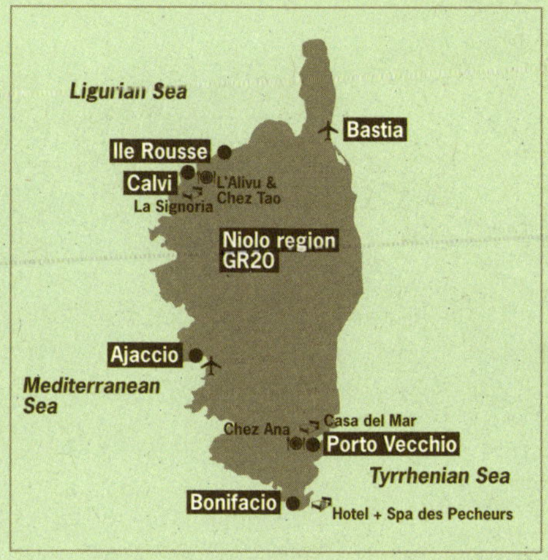

Regional Information

The Greeks called Corsica, 'Kalliste' that literally means 'most beautiful'. More recently it has been called, 'the mountain in the sea,' 'the fragrant isle' or the 'granite isle' or the French happen to call it 'La Corse' whichever name you feel is most apt, Corsica will captivate you with its stunning rugged beauty. This gem of an island seems to rise out of the sea, with the peak of Monte Cinto topping the island at 2,716 meters above sea level. Corsica is the fourth largest island in the Mediterranean and is also the highest, with an average altitude of 680 meters above sea level. Rugged mountain ranges, forests and a thousand-kilometre coastline all offer breathtaking scenery ideal for those looking for a more active honeymoon with walking, scuba-diving, cycling and world-class windsurfing on your doorstep. Corsica isn't just for action heroes, the beaches are undeniably pretty too with intimate golden coves and clear azure sea perfect for couples wanting peace and relaxation.

Located between France and Italy, just north of Sardinia, Corsica seems to have remained relatively unchanged for generations; its wild countryside, crumbling fortresses and clean beaches make it appear imaginary. Perhaps one of the reasons why it may be unspoilt is the inaccessibility. Although the island is fairly well served by ferry companies from nearby Sardinia, mainland France and Italy, the ferries are seasonal and can take several hours. Although, if you happen to be visiting nearby Sardinia, Mobylines offer an excellent service between pretty Santa Teresa di Gallura and the fortress town of Bonifacio. The main airline operators to the island are Air France and Compagnie Corse Mediteranée which run flights to Ajaccio, Bastia, Calvi and Figari but you will have to connect through one of the mainland French airports. Getting around Corsica can be almost as tricky as getting to it. Despite the four airports on the island, you can't fly internally, so be prepared to get out on the roads. Hiring a moped or bike are popular, exciting ways of exploring the countryside, although in major towns simply walking around is easy enough.

Adventure: Action
Destination: Corsica

Corsica's is renowned for its superb hiking trails most of which take up the 330,000 hectares of the Parc Naturel Regional including the legendary GR20 also known as Fra Li Monti (meaning between the mountains). You can hike the GR20 (or at least some of it) during the summer months from mid-June to October. In Ajaccio itself the 'Maison d'informations Randonees' sells a few walking guides, if you are brave enough to do it yourself, or if you are not feeling confident, book an organised tour with 'Objectif Nature' a locally-run company based in Bastia who arrange guided cycling, hiking and horse riding trips to part of the GR20.

Towns on the island like Bonifacio, Bastia and Ajaccio with their museums, galleries, churches, boutiques and historical centres provide wonderful points for exploration. Bonifacio has a beautiful old town perched high on a 70-metre cliff overlooking the picturesque harbour, littered with millionaire yachts, gorgeous boutiques and bistros. The cliff top citadel is a charming maze of alleyways with a distinct mediaeval feel, on a clear day you may well see as far as Sardinia. Bustling Bastia is Corsica's main centre of business and commerce and has a very Italian atmosphere reminiscent of its colourful past. You may find spending a day just wandering around the Old Port enough. If you are looking for a wild and scenic drive then there is no-where better than the Ajaccio to Calvi coastal route - it'll take you a few hours but its well worth it. Ajaccio itself is a fabulous historical town with plenty of museums and churches to explore. Calvi is an excellent spot for sunbathing on sandy beaches, learning to scuba dive or listening the live music during the infamous jazz festival, which is held every June.

If you happen to be staying in one of the towns and you want to explore the mountainous regions, then 'Aiguilles de Bavella', also called the Bavella Needles, an immense peak district area. Peaks, which rise to a height of more than 1600 metres (5250ft) also known as the 'Cornes d'Asinao' (Asinao Horns), are a wonderful place for climbing, canyoning and walking. There is a high-mountain spur of the GR20 that splits off beyond 'Notre Dame des Neiges' and allows you to approach the peaks.

For beach lovers, water sports enthusiasts and worshippers there are plenty of stretches of sandy beaches and hidden coves throughout Corsica. Some of the best are found around the Calvi region and Ile Rousse, where you'll find plenty of sun-loungers and companies eager to take you on fishing trips. Out of Calvi town you'll find 'Lama' where there is a gorgeous white crescent shaped sandy beach called 'Lozari' which is more relaxed. In the North West the top beaches 'Loto' and 'Saleccia' are accessible only by foot and they are incredibly peaceful even during the summer months. Palombaggio in the South towards prestigious town of Port Vecchio is perhaps the most famous on the island, it has beautiful white sand and the water is very clear, wheras Sant Guilia is the most popular spot for watersports, with cafés and bars lining the area.

Top. The swimming pool and views at Casa del Mar. **Bottom.** Fine French cuisine.

Stylish Places to Stay

Super deluxe: Casa del Mar. A splendid, luxurious and very romantic retreat, perfectly situated in the upmarket town of Porto Vecchio. Highlights are the infinity pool and excellent restaurant; perfect for those looking for a relaxing honeymoon without the pretence.

Garden chic: La Signoria. Original historical building with antique furnishings, vaulted ceiling set in pristine, luscious gardens. Calvi centre is only 5km away so the location is perfect for those who want to explore the town by night or day.

Island beach chic: Hotel & Spa des Pecheurs. Fantastic secluded location with secluded beach setting and the only way to get around is by golf cart. The 50-room hotel has been built out of typical local rock, which may sound like an eco-lodge but in fact it is elegant, luxurious and charming.

Delicious Places to Eat

Corsican folk charm: Chez Tao. Located in Calvi, this ochre-coloured 16th century spot, offers excellent seafood, but the food is secondary to the atmosphere of Corsican folk singing and piano, as well as the presence of the occasional celebrity. The owners are said to be direct descendents of Rasputin.

Italian delight: Chez Ana. Famed for its perfect Italian cuisine, especially the stuffed aubergines, fresh gnocchi and lasagne. Located off the main square of Porto Vecchio near the Hotel de Ville.

Haute cuisine: L'Alivu. This famed restaurant prepares authentic French and continental cuisine and has a Michelin star rating by the eminent French restaurant guide. The seasonal delicacies in the restaurant are prepared by a dedicated gourmet team headed by Christophe Bacquie. Dress to impress at this special, lavish restaurant.

Opposite page. Top. Beach Plage, Antibes. **Bottom.** Monaco view.

Adventure: Culture + Art
Destination: Cote d'azur

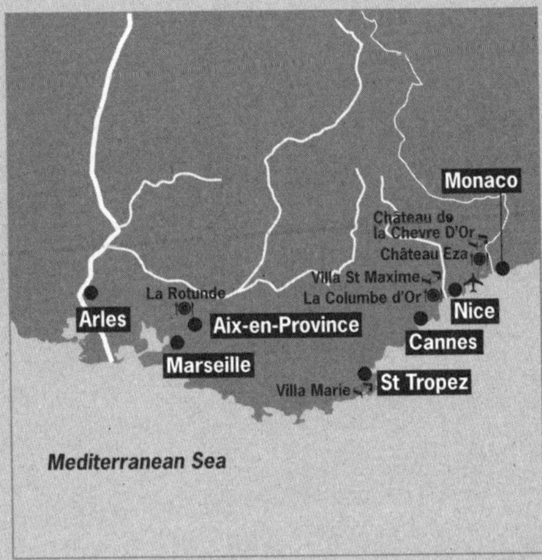

Regional Information

French people take their culture very seriously, and the evidence of this passion for their country and heritage is expressed through the many galleries devoted to the fashion industry, a number of renowned art museums in the cities, and cinematic festivals. France's heritage in the arts is particularly rich, as the country is able to boast names such as Henri Matisse, Vincent Van Gogh, Albert Camus, and Victor Hugo, among a host of others. The French hold fêtes (celebrations, or festivals) throughout the year, which can certainly add to the cultural experience of any visitor to this country, and will enliven the atmosphere of your own honeymoon celebration.

The province region is full of artistic charm, and pretty villages full of locals drinking pastis and playing petanque rather than bus loads of tourists. The charm of Arles is a wonderful treat for those who enjoy art and café culture. The 'art trail' as it's known hosts a list of exceptional homegrown artistic talent and an impressive array of world-class galleries; France has a phenomenal artistic heritage. Musee d'Arles et de la Province Antiques located opposite the remains of the Cirque Romain was inaugurated in 1995, and is an outstanding museum of ancient history filled with roman relics and sarcophagi. La Ferme des Collettes is one of Renoirs most famous pieces depicting a warm sunny day in the South of France, visit the stunning Mansion in cagnes-sur-mer where the artist previously lived which is now Musee Renoir. Musee Picasso is packed with paintings from Picasso's time spent at Château Grimaldini in Antibes and views of the Mediterranean. Finally who can forget the famous Van Gogh who depicted scenes from Arles in beautiful colour? The Fondation de Van Gogh displays a wealth of paintings from international artists inspired by Van Gogh. Art enthusiats will love perusing around the pretty Palais de Luppe where the Van Gogh tribute is displayed. Every June the Fetes d'Arles (festival) kicks off with dance, theatre and poetry hitting the streets which can be a very special time to visit for anyone.

BEACH - PLAGE
Bar - Restaurant - Grill
Beach Plage

Opposite page. Top. Poolside at Château de La Chevre d'Or. Bottom. View from Château Eza.

Adventure: Culture + Art
Destination: Cote d'azur

Relaxing outside a café watching the world go by can be a real treat anywhere in France, but especially in the province region. The café culture is most prominent, and no-where more than the famous Café Jardin Delices at the Espace Van Gogh, overlooking ornamental gardens that inspired the famous artist. The very yellow Café Van Gogh produced the inspiration for Café at night scene, which invariably does get busy, but is well worth an espresso or two.

If the art scene overwhelms you, then the food in the Province region is delightful. The bustling markets of Arles, and the famous Aix-en-province are renowned for their luscious fruit and vegetables and regional varieties of cheese, olives and fresh bread. They are perfect for picking up a picnic before heading out on the road or just soaking up the local atmosphere. There is also a wonderful Flower market in Aix-en-province too, which might be just the place to pick up a lovely bouquet for your loved one as a special honeymoon surprise.

The Cote d'Azur, also known as the French Rivera stretches along France's Mediterranean coastline from Toulon to the Italian border. You could easily spend a week or two in this region alone exploring the main towns and capital Nice, however St Tropez is the cream of the crop. The cobblestone courtyards, sleek yachts and lavish homes filled with designer fashion make it a bit of a jet-set location. If you want to really pull out all the stops on your honeymoon, you may well hire a yacht for the day and sail around the coastline drinking champagne and topping up your tan like the rich locals.

Cote d'Azur is also renowned globally for its film festivals, art galleries and famous museums. Staged on the Cote d'Azur since 1939 and famed for its lavish after parties the glamorous, star-studded Cannes Film Festival has become one of the greatest showcases in the world for innovative, ultramodern moviemakers and critics. Although there have been few French movies that have reached 'Hollywood's' level of commercial success, French filmmakers still proceed to produce some 200 films a year. Visitors might not be lucky enough to get invited to one of the lavish parties, but if you happen to be in Cannes during the festival you'll love the bustling atmosphere.

Stylish Places to Stay

Riviera style: Villa Marie, Ramatuelle. A small boutique hotel with acres of pine & cypress trees, situated only 2 miles from St Tropez, so an excellent location for those wanting both a haven to relax or to explore the nightlife of St Tropez. Highlights include the own-product spa, 1940's French antique furniture and the best pastries on the Rivieria.

Medieval empire: Château De la Chevre D'Or. Romantic Old World Inn, once a medieval castle, perched high on a hillside with magnificent coastal views.

Modern Province chic: Villa Saint Maxime. A glass enclosed atrium welcomes you into this chic retreat, nestled beneath the ramparts of the ancient, fortified city of St. Paul de Vence. With stunning views overlooking the Mediterranean, the Cap d'Antibes, and the Alpes Maritimes, this is a perfectly small boutique hotel with a very personal feel.

Delicious Places to Eat

Terrace chic: La Colombe d'Or, Tables covered in white linen and situated in a private courtyard, which is dotted by original artwork. During the film festival the restaurant buzzes with famous people, so can be difficult to get a reservation. But totally worth it for its good quality French cuisine.

Panoramic views: Château Eza. A 10-minute hike up the cobblestone path lead you to Eza. A glorious Michelin star restaurant which is built into the rock giving panoramic views over the coast. They offer a 3-course lunch menu 'fixee' for about 80 Euros.

Provincial perfect: La Rotonde. Located on Place de la Rotonde overlooking the pretty fountain, a great place, hip and attracting a young crowd, of course only "les jeunes avec l'argent". The cuisine is innovative, serving Provençal dishes with a touch of fusion cuisine. Definitely a place to eat very well, to see and be seen.

Opposite page. Château les Crayeres.

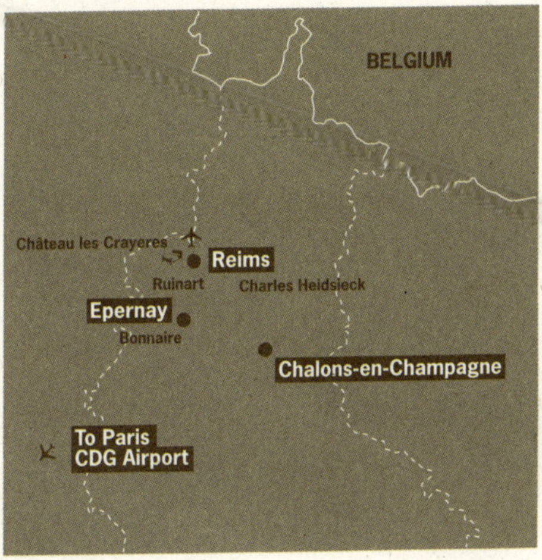

Focus On...
Champagne tasting

France has been regarded as the world's premier wine-producing nation since the middle ages – even though the competition from the upstart of 'new world wines' has challenged its monopoly – wine is still very much the heart of France and French culture. Champagne is consumed by the French and everyone else worldwide as a celebratory drink and for some lucky few, a regular drink.

During the 17th century monk Dom Pérignon, the famous cellar-master of the Abbey of Hautvilliers, taught the wine growers the secrets of Champagne. He did not create, but perfected the art of 'mousse' (the bubbles) by using a second fermentation process to create the carbon dioxide. The process may well be replicated throughout the world but no-where can claim the name 'Champagne' unless it is produced in the Champagne region. You may see "methode champenoise" on some sparkling wines which means that it basically follows the same processes as the one used to produce Champagne but this wine has derived from another region. A trip to the Champagne region is a special treat for anyone interested in the production, the rolling vineyards and tasting sessions. Reims (one of the major tourist towns) is only an hour from Paris, so anyone staying in Paris can hop over for the day or better still stay a few nights and soak up the atmosphere. There are several companies (such as Grape Escapes) that also offer personal tours, which are a good option for both honeymooners wanting exclusivity or for hen and stag parties.

There are several 'champagne' maisons (houses) in the region that are open for 'tastings and tours', although most have to be booked in advance; like the famous and spectacular Château de Bligny (one of the few houses producing on site) or the fabulous and family fun Bonnaire. Other appointment-only maisons are Ruinart, Charles Heidsieck, and Lanson. Finally, to get an overview of the various champagnes available (plus wines from all over France), it's worth visiting La Vino Cave, where you can also buy all the paraphernalia of the bubbly business, from champagne flutes to snazzy servers.

If you do chose to stay the night then Château Les Crayeres, located in Reims is an extremely elegant 2-story Château situated in luscious and private landscaped gardens, and only staggering distance from nearby champagne houses Veuve Cliquet and Pommery.

Stylish Essentials

General Information

Airlines

Air France
www.airfrance.co.uk
T. 0870 142 4343 (UK reservations)

British Airways
www.ba.com
T. 0844 493 0 787 (UK reservations & enquiries)

BMI
www.flybmi.com
T. 0870 6070 555 (UK reservations & enquiries)

Trains

Eurostar
www.eurostar.com
T. 08705 186 186 (UK bookings)

Rail Europe
For all train tickets across Europe (including TGV)
www.raileurope.co.uk

Paris Metro Information
www.ratp.info

Cycling Tours

Deluxe Cycle Tours
www.deluxecycletours.com
T. +44 (0)1926 334216 (UK)
T. +33 (0)5 53 51 26 90 (France)
E. info@deluxecycletours.com

Paris

Musee D'Orsay
On Leftbank opposite Tuileries Gardens
www.musee-orsay.fr
Entrance is on Rue de la Legion d'Honneur
M° Solferino

Arc de Triomphe
Open: Daily 10.00–22.30 (23.00 in summer)
Tickets cost €8 and must be bought 30 minutes before closing.
M° Charles de Gaulle-Etoile

Eiffel Tower
www.tour-eiffel.fr
Open: Daily 9.00–0.00 (last entrance 23.00)
M° Trocadero or Ecole Militaire

Classic Walks
Da Vinci Code Tour of Paris
www.classicwalksparis.com
T. +33 (0) 156 58 10 54
E. info@classicwalksparis.com

La Colette
213 rue Saint-Honoré - 75001 Paris
www.colette.fr
T. +33 (0) 155 35 33 90
F. +33 (0) 155 35 33 99
Open: from Monday to Saturday 11.00–19.00
M° Tuileries or Pyramides

Galeries Lafayette
40, boulevard Haussmann -75009 Paris
www.galerieslafayette.com
T. +33 (0) 142 82 34 56
Open: Monday to Saturday from 9:30–19:30
M° Chaussee D'Antin

Lenôtre Cooking School & café
Pastries for picnics, coffees and cooking
www.lenotre.fr
T.+ 33 (0) 142 65 97 60 (information & reservations)

Hotel Kube – Ice Bar
1-5, passage Ruelle, 75018 Paris
www.kubehotel.com
T. + 33 (0) 142 05 2000
F. + 33 (0) 142 05 21 01
M° Place de Clichy

Lizard Lounge
18, rue du Bourg-Tibourg, 75004 Paris
T. +33 (0) 142 72 81 34
M° Hotel de Ville

VIP Room
78 Avenue Champs-Elysées, 75008 Paris
T. +33 (0) 156 69 16 66
M° Franklin-D.-Roosevelt

Panoramic Bar
3 Place du Général Koenig, 75017 Paris
T. +33 (0) 140 68 50 68
M° Porte Maillot

George V
31, Avenue George V, 75008 Paris
www.fourseasons.com/paris/
T. +33 (0) 149 52 70 00
M° George V

Hotel Keppler
10 Rue Kepler, Paris, 75116 Paris
www.keppler-paris-hotel.com
T. +33 (0) 147 20 65 05
M° George V

La Villa Paris
33, rue de la Fontaine a Mulard, 75013 Paris
www.la-villa-paris.com
T. +33 (0) 143 47 15 66
M° Place d'Italie

Lasserre
17 Av Franklin Roosevelt, 75008 Paris
T. +33 (0) 143 59 02 13
www.restaurant-lasserre.com
Open: Monday to Saturday 19.00–22.00
M° Franklin D Roosevelt

Le Patio Provencal
116 rue des Dames, 17th quarter, Paris
T. +33 (0) 142 93 73 73
Open: Daily
M° Villiers

Ma Bourgogne
19 Place des Vosges, 4th quarter, Paris
T. +33 (0) 142 78 44 64
Open: Daily from 8.00–1.30
M° Bastille

Corsica

Airlines

Compagnie Corse Mediteranée
www.ccm-airlines.com

Moby Lines ferries
www.mobylines.it
T. +49 (0) 61114 020 (helpline)

GR20
Open: Early June - Mid October
10 days needed

Maison d'Informations Randonees
Parc Naturel Regional de la Corse
2 Rue Major Lambroschini, Ajaccio
T. +33 (0) 495 51 79 10
Open: 8.30–12:30 and 14.00–18.00

Objectif Nature
3 Rue Notre Dame de Lourdes, Bastia
www.objectif-nature-corse.com
T. +33 (0) 495 32 54 34

World Walks
GR20 Self-guided itineraries
www.worldwalks.com
T. 01242 254 353 (UK)

Walking Holidays

Headwater
www.headwater.com
T. 08700 662650 (UK)

Walks Worldwide
www.walksworldwide.com
T. 01524 242000 (UK)

Calvi Jazz festival
www.calvi-jazz-festival.com
E. info@calvi-jazz-festival.com

Scuba Diving
Visit www.padi.com for a complete list of diving schools

E.P.I.C. Padi 5 star Dive Centre
Villa les Muiers, Rte de Pietramaggiore, Calvi
www.epic-plongee.com
T. +33 (0) 613386126

Casa Del Mar
Route de Palombaggia BP 93
20538 Porto-Vecchio, South Corsica
www.casadelmar.fr/english/
T. +33 (0) 495 72 34 34

La Signoria
Route De La Foret De Bonifato,
20260 Calvi
www.hotel-la-signoria.com
T. +33 (0) 495 65 93 00

Hotel & Spa des Pecheurs
Ile de Cavallo, Bonifacio
www.hoteldespecheurs.com
T. +33 (0) 495 70 36 39

Chez Tao
La Citadelle, 20260, Calvi
www.cheztao.com
T. +33 (0) 495 65 0073
Open: 13.00–04.00

Chez Anna
Rue Doct de Rocca Serra 20137,
Porto Vecchio
T. +33 (0) 495 70 19 97
Open:

L'Alivu – Hotel La Villa
Chemin Notre Dame de la Serra, Calvi
www.hotel-lavilla.com
T. +33 (0) 495 65 10 10
Open: Evening dinner only

Province & Cote d'Azur

Local information
www.guideriviera.com

Musée départemental de l'Arles antiques
Presqu'île-du-cirque-romain BP 205 -
13635 Arles cedex
www.arles-antique.org
T. +33 (0) 490 18 88 88
E. info.mapa@cg13.fr
Open: Daily 09.00–19.00 (April to October) 10.00–17.00 (November to March)

Art Galleries

Fondation Van Gogh
www.fondationvangogh-arles.org/
T. +33 (0) 490 49 94 04

Musee Matisse
164, av. des Arènes de Cimiez
06000 Nice.
www.musee-matisse-nice.org
T. +33 (0) 493 81 08 08

Musée Picasso
Château Grimaldi 06600 Antibes
www.antibes-juanlespins.com/fr/culture/musees/picasso
T. +33 (0) 492 90 54 20

Fete D'Arles
35 Place de la Republique
www.fetes-arles.com
T. +33 (0) 490 96 47 00

Café Jardin Delices
Espace Van Gogh

Café Van Gogh
Place du Forum

Yacht Hire
Hire a yacht in St Tropez, Nice or Antibes
www.aquacruise.com/yacht_hire

Cannes Film Festival
www.festival-cannes.fr

The Festival d'Art Pyrotechnique
Six-night firework extravaganza.
www.festival-pyrotechnique-cannes.com

Markets

Aix-en-Province
Open: Saturday 9.00–00.30

Marseille
Open: Sunday 8.00–19.00

Flower Market Aix-en-Province
Place de Precheurs
Open: Sunday mornings

Place de l'Hotel de Ville
Open: Tuesday and Saturday mornings

La Colombe d'Or
Place du General de Gaulle
www.la-colombe-dor.com
T. +33 (0) 493 32 80 02
E. contact@la-colombe-dor.com

Château Eza
Rue de la Pise
www.chateaueza.com
T. +33 (0) 493 41 12 24

La Rotonde
2A place Jeanne D'Arc, Aix-en-Province
www.larotonde-aix.com
T. +33 (0) 442 91 61 70
Open: 20.00–02.00

Villa St Maxime
390 Route de la Colle, St. Paul de Vence
www.villa-st-maxime.com
T. +33 (0) 493 32 7600
E. riviera@villa-st-maxime.com

Château De la Chevre D'Or
Moyenne corniche, rue du Barri
06360 EZE-VILLAGE
www.chevredor.co
T. + 33 (0) 492 10 66 66

Reims

Tourist information in Epernay
7 Avenue de Champagne
Epernay
www.ot-epernay.fr
T. +33 (0) 326 53 33 00

Grape Escapes
Wine & Champagne Tours
& Accommodation
www.grapeescapes.net
T. 0 8707 667 617 (UK)

Private Tour of Château de Bligny
T. +33 (0) 325 27 40 11

Bonnaire Champagne
120 rue d'Epernay 51350 Cramant
www.champagne-bonnaire.com
T. +33 (0) 326 57 50 85
F. +33 (0) 326 57 59 17

Alghero sunset, Sardinia.

ITALY

Venice | Dolomites | Sardinia | Milan |

ITALY

Why is this place so special?

What's not to love about Italy? Its romantic landscapes, stylish cities, stunning architecture and importantly the warm and friendly people. You could keep on visiting Italy for the rest of your life and never exhaust all that it has to offer. The country synonymous with romance boasts a rich tradition of lovers, from the saucy ancient counsel of Ovid to the excesses of Latino lover Casanova (who claimed to have slept with 122 women in his autobiography). Italy means something different to everybody – gigantic pizza's, homemade gelati (ice cream), hot beaches and speeding vespa's. One thing that everyone can agree on is Italy's romantic reputation.

Venice maybe a clichéd destination for honeymooners its iconic canal ways, gondolas and cathedrals make it certainly special and unique. Spending a day or two perusing around the ornamental palaces, or partake in the famous Venetian masked ball can be an incredible adventure. However, if you have already been to Italy's big tourist destinations and are looking for something off-the-beaten track – the 'Dolomites' are a splendid destination for couples wanting action adventure and picturesque scenery. This mountainous region is equally stunning in both the summer and the winter with plenty of outdoor activities to keep you entertained. For unspoilt beaches, rock pools, caves and glorious sunsets head towards Sardinia; its stunning rugged coastline, historical sites and quaint village towns, may feel a million miles away from the powerhouse pace of Milan with a laidback and slower tempo.

Top. St. Marks Square, Venice. **Bottom.** Santa Teresa, Sardinia.

Often in Italy you will find the more you travel off the major tourist trail the warmer the welcome. Italians are invariably proud of their local towns and surroundings, and they will be delighted and flattered if you take an interest, especially if it's a special occasion like your honeymoon and you have chosen it to stay in their town. If you hear locals saying 'Tanti Auguri' which literally means 'good wishes' – they are wishing you a happy life together.

Italy is a fabulous choice for seriously romantic honeymoon couples and accommodation is vast from family run farmhouses to opulent Palazzo's. You can spend as little or as much as your pocket can afford. As it's only 2 or 3 hours from the UK if you are short on time or don't want to travel long-haul then you can still experience a special romantic honeymoon without breaking the bank.

Fast Facts

Capital: Rome.

Location: Italy is instantly recognizable by its boot shape, which is surrounded by the Adriatic, Ionian, Ligurian and Tyrrhenian Seas - all of which form part of the Mediterranean Sea. The Alps separate Italy from France, Switzerland, Austria and Slovenia.

Population: 58,462,375.

Religion: 84% Roman Catholic, 16% other (Protestants, Jews and Muslims).

Languages: Standard Italian and numerous dialects are spoken.

Opposite page. From top. Secluded beach in Sardinia, Venice canal, Sardinia, Santa Teresa.

Getting there and exploring around

Getting to Italy from the UK or the rest of Europe is relatively easy. There are many direct and low-cost flights to Italy from the UK, such as Rynair, Easjet and ThomsonFly. Alitalia is the national airline, and flies direct from the UK to both Rome and Milan. British Airways and BMI fly directly from London to Naples. Many of the routes change with the seasons, so it is always best to check online. The Orient Express train takes four days from London via Paris and Venice to Rome, if you want to do it in style and linger over the beautiful scenery, then this is the way to travel.

Getting around Italy by car is the most flexible and fun. Roads are generally good, and there is an excellent network of freeways, although you do have to pay tolls. Be careful in the major cities like Milan, the roads and parking is a nightmare, and it's better to stick to public transport or walk. Domestic air travel can be costly and is probably worth doing only if you are really short of time.

Ferry services link Italy's mainland to its islands; Sicily from Naples, Civitavecchia, Reggio di Calabria, Livorno and Genoa, while Sardinia can be reached from Genoa, La Spezia, Civitavecchia, Livorno, Naples, Tràpani and Palermo, or from Corsica to Sardinia with locally run ferries usually every hour. You can book ahead online before to save time queuing.

Best time of year to visit

Summer temperatures in the South are far hotter than in the North – especially in the mountain regions, which have heavy winter snowfalls. The North is also the wettest area, and heavy rainfall tends to be between October and December. The best time to visit the Dolomites is when everything is open from mid-July through to September, and the weather is pleasant. However from January to April, is also a fantastic time for skiers, as the snow has fallen and all the mountain lifts are open.

The rest of Italy is at its best in spring (April-May) and autumn (October-November). During these seasons, the scenery is beautiful, the temperature pleasant and there are usually fewer crowds.

Try to avoid August, as this is the time when most Italians take their vacations, known as 'la ferragosta', and many shops and businesses are closed as a result. However on the islands it's a busy time to visit, so pre-booking accommodation is absolutely essential

? Must know before you go

Looking the part. In Italy, where image is everything and baring skin anywhere but the beach will welcome wolf whistles, comments and stares; dress modestly, especially when visiting churches, (the heart of many Italian communities). If the church guardian deems your dress is inappropriate they won't let you in.

Feeding time. To eat and drink in Italy is an integral part and the heart of Italian life. Although Italy has exported its pizza's and pasta's around the globe, 'cucina Italiana' (typical Italian Cuisine) doesn't really exist. What you will find on your travels though is regional cuisine, such as Sardinian 'Malloreddus alla campidanese' – a country style pasta dish with sausage sauce.

Baci (kisses). Public displays of affection are pretty normal it Italy. Italians greet friends with two light kisses on the cheek, first the right and then the left. Even if you're merely acquaintances, this form of greeting is usual, both on arrival and departure. However on first introduction a handshake is usual, although not necessarily the firm businesslike shake other nationalities may be used to.

Highlights

Seductive history. Sample Venice's romantic canal ways and listen to tales of the historic city on a nightly ghost walk.

Mulled wine and sightseeing. Trek, ski and drink Glüehwein in the scenic Dolomites region.

Sun, Sea and Sandcastles. Bathe in clear waters, sun yourself on pristine white beaches and explore the historical remains of Sardinia.

Shopping in Milan. Stroll down any of the Milanese streets and experience the epitome of Italian elegance, glamour and killer heels.

Tip for the Trip

"Head to off-the-beaten track destinations, even if it's just for a night or two. There will be fewer couples on their honeymoon and its likely you will get a better service, a warmer welcome and it will feel more special rather just following the crowd."

Jill

Opposite page. Top. Venice canal.
Bottom. Venice, St. Marks Square.

Adventure: Culture + Art
Destination: Venice

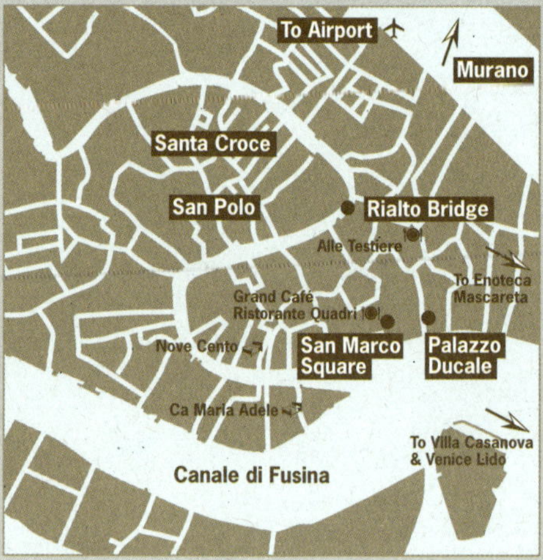

Regional Information

Venice (Venezia) needs no introduction. Venice, 'la Serenissima', (the most serene) is Italy's floating jewel, the destination that comes closest to an incarnation of romance. It may be a clichéd destination for honeymooners, but few can resist the romantic appeal of a midnight gondola ride, a wander hand-in-hand over the Bridge of Sighs or if you brave enough delving into the enchanting past during a midnight ghost walk. The perfect place for that romantic trip and a place you'll hope to tell the grandchildren all about.

Venice is a glorious cliché, more romantic, more beautiful and more surprising than you could expect. No matter how many photographs or films you may have seen, it is still a jaw-dropping experience seeing Venice's canals, palaces and cathedrals for the first time. That first cruise down the Grand Canal is one of life's unforgettable experiences. The gondola rides although quite expensive (you can try and haggle) are worth every penny. You don't really need to 'book' a gondola (although this can be arranged at San Marco, Rialto or the train station) just head to the nearest jetty on one of the main canals.

The main tourist magnet in Venice is the 'Piazza San Marco', better known to Anglophones as St. Mark's Square. It is a popular spot for watching the world go by with a café espresso and what's more, the square is bordered by historic buildings (such as the Doge's Palace and the Basilica) and represents the focal point of Venice's water transport system. The Palazzo Ducale (Ducal Palace, also known as Doge's Palace) was the residence of the Doge up to the fall of the Venetian Republic in 1797, a public palace and seat of the administration of justice. All historic periods are represented in an extraordinary stratification of structural and decorative elements: from the antique foundations of the original Gothic complex, to the great halls dedicated to political life and decorated by the canvases of Veronese.

Adventure: Culture + Art
Destination: Venice

The Venice Basilica, built in the 9th century, maintains the characteristic profile of a typical Byzantine church. It is the principal church in Venice and was the place where the Doges were ordained. Both attractions may be visited independently, but if you prefer, hire a local tour guide to take you around.

Venice's quietest season is winter. You're unlikely to find Venice empty of tourists at any time, but late autumn and the first part of the winter are the best times to come if you want to avoid the crowds and take advantage of cheaper hotel rates. This is the best time to see a (relatively) tourist-free Venice - but be prepared for icy temperatures and mists. In January and February the two-week-long Carnival is one of Venice's big attractions and the crowds flock in - it is even more important at this time to book a hotel well in advance. There are masks and parties; it's a bit tamer now, though, than the decadent excesses of the past. If you happen to miss the Venice carnival, then there is a fabulous Venvice Carnival Show (in English) at the theatre at San Marco, the story is about a family of mask makers and costumiers, and a pre-theatre Venetian dinner, which makes this a lovely evening out.

As the spring turns into summer, tourist numbers rise; and Venice in the height of summer is avoided by many. August can also be swelteringly hot, so if you arrive at this time of year, make sure your hotel, at least, has air conditioning. The Venice Film Festival is a cultural treat, and this takes place in late August and early September, swarming with the film industry's glitterati – its Italy's version of Cannes.

Venice is composed of more than a hundred tiny islets, packed closely together around canals. The city is in a lagoon, protected from the sea by a long strip of land called the Lido. Venice is famously sinking. Every year high water levels threaten the city's fabric, and it has long been feared that the beautiful city will one day disappear beneath the water. Many ideas (and funds) have been put forward to protect the endangered heritage site, but the problem is a complex one and 'solutions', such as to construct a giant water gate, are controversial. Today you'll see water taxis slowing down, as the government appears to have installed speed cameras to encourage slow movements and fewer waves that may increase erosion.

Murano, a cluster of 5 islets, linked by bridges and only a few minutes from Venice, is home to the famous glass blowing factories. The Venetian glassware can be seen in workshops, and just wandering around the canals, taking in the views is equally incredible. It's a miniature version of Venice and is much more peaceful. Visiting the galleries and showrooms on Murano, and the island's glass museums and leading churches are the main highlights.

There are many budget flights from the UK now, so if you're looking for an economic elopement rather than a leisurely luxury honeymoon, Venice is an ideal option. Its also perfect as a stop over for a couple of nights before exploring other parts of Italy.

Below from left. Nove Cento, bedroom at Nove Cento, Grand Café Ristorante Quadri.

Stylish Places to Stay

Chic Retreat: Ca Maria Adele. A lavish 16th century palazzo, with a fabulous location overlooking the Grand Canal and 300 metres from St Mark's Square. Take an evening aperitif on the hotel terrace, with its sumptuous scatter of oriental silk cushions and Moroccan-inspired decor. Opt for 'The Doge's Room' with lavish red damask walls, chandeliers and gilt-edged mirrors.

Eclectic Charm: Nove Cento. A 9-room charming boutique gem tucked down an alley close to San Marco square, the Grand Canal and the Gritti Palace. The friendly staff and the library give it a relaxing and charming atmosphere.

Eco Chic: Villa Casanova. All rooms at the Feng-Shui-designed Villa Casanova in Venice are made with natural materials; cork, slaked lime, travertino marble and oil-polished wooden floors. Book the four-poster romantic room for an ultra-romantic retreat.

Delicious Places to Eat

Seafood in style: Alle Testiere. A strong local following can make it tough to get one of the 22 seats at this tiny trattoria near Campo Santa Maria Formosa. Varied fish dishes from Monkfish to Swordfish are its specialties as are the delicious desserts such as fig and almond cake. The owner and staff are very warm and attentive.

Special Romance: Grand Café Ristorante Quadri. Founded in 1775 as a Turkish khava (coffee) house by one Giorgio Quadri from Corfu. The coffee house remains among the porticos on the ground floor, while the grand first floor restaurant was created in 1830. The seasoned Italian dishes and the stunning candlelit views over San Marco make this an excellent romantic dining spot.

Platters & Wine: Enoteca Mascareta. Mauro Lorenzon, an actor and wine connoisseur, keeps a serious cave with champagne and wine by the glass, although only open for dinner, it regularly draws in locals until 2am. Try to cured meats and cheese platters for a real local treat.

Opposite page, clockwise from top left.
View of Dolomites, walking in the Dolomites, Hanging bridge via ferrata Ivano Dibano.

Adventure: Action
Destination: Dolomites

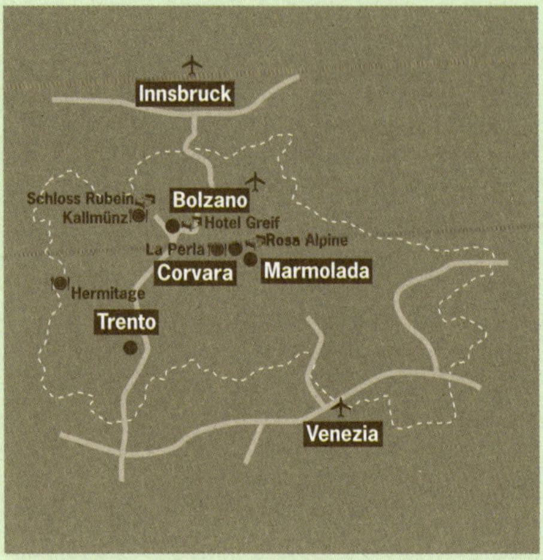

Regional Information

The autonomous Alpine region known as 'The Dolomites' located in northern Italy, include three main areas and bounded by the regional borders of Veneto, Trentino Alto Adige and Friuli. Alto Adige or South Tirol in the North was a part of the Tirolo province of Austria until ceded to Italy in 1918. The people, mostly of German descent are tri-lingual, speaking German 68%, Italian 28% and Ladin 4%.

Bolzano airport in the region is only served by European flights, alternatively the nearest airports are Verona and Innesbruck. By car, from Milan it would take 4 hours to drive to the mountains, from Munich 3 and a half hours and Venice an hour and a half. You can also reach the Dolomites by train on the main line crossing the Brenner Pass and connecting Austria with major Italian cities. Fortezza train station is an ideal departure point for people wanting to visit the northern section of the Dolomites, while Bolzano would probably be the most convenient for the southern parts of the mountain range.

The Dolomites region is filled with outdoor activities for those seeking an active honeymoon, from walking, bike-riding, climbing and skiing; and for those not so active the region is wonderfully picturesque and the après-ski poses fabulous nightlife for music lovers.

Most visitors tend to flock here during the Winter months, when the region is covered in white snow; and skiing, winter hiking, ice-skating and sledging are popular activities. For more than a century the Dolomites have been one of the most developed and historically important centres for winter sports in the world. The Dolomites offer perfect pistes for all levels of ability, evocative cross country circuits, impressive ice stadiums, some of the most beautiful ski mountaineering itineraries in the Alps, short walks and long winter hikes, breathtaking off-piste descents and an infinite number of other possibilities that include all the valleys in the Dolomites.

Adventure: Action
Destination: Dolomites

The Dolomiti Superski carousel is the jewel in the crown of what's on offer in the Dolomites: 1200 km of pistes, 460 lifts and 475 interconnected pistes. A single ski pass is all that is needed for this immense 12 valley winter carousel; from Cortina d'Ampezzo to Plan de Corones in the Alta Badia, from Val Gardena and the Alpe di Siusi to Val di Fassa and Carezza, to Arabba, Alta Val Pusteria and Val di Fiemme. And from San Martino di Castrozza and Passo Rolle to Valle dell'Isarco, the Tre Valli, the Civetta group and the newest addition, the Marmolada, Queen of the Dolomites.

During the Summer months when the flowers are in full-bloom and there are longer daylight days, it is ideal for fell-walking, mountain biking and climbing. From alpinism to sports climbing, routes of all types and grades exist, weaving their way up an infinite number of splendid rock faces, seemingly created for what here in the Dolomites has historically been one of the major sports. And then there are of course the 'Vie Ferrate' and equipped paths, 'invented' here, enabling easy access to the summits of the greatest and highest Dolomite peaks. The Dolomites are also a paradise for mountain bikers, as they offer many different itineraries for cyclists of all abilities. To fully enjoy the silence and fabulous panoramas of some of the most famous mountains, you can choose from the many paths designated specifically to mountain bikers, whilst remembering not to ride on those reserved for hikers. The important Alte Vie have been created specifically for trekkers and hikers: these long itineraries cross through entire Dolomite groups and allow for an in-depth understanding of the area as, day after day, walkers come into direct contact with nature and the mountains themselves. The close-knit and varied network of paths, be they long and difficult or short and simple, offer all walkers the possibility of enjoying the forests, rock faces, rivers, lakes and the outstanding beauty of the Monti Pallidi, the Pale Mountains. The mountain guides, based in every village in the Dolomites, will of course be pleased to offer advice and accompany you in complete safety throughout all these activities.

For those wishing to feel the emotions that only flying can offer there are many specialised schools and centres. Beginners and experts alike can choose from paragliding and hang-gliding to admire forests and steep mountain faces from up high. Water sports such as canoeing, kayaking, rafting, sailing and windsurfing can all be carried out in this region comprised of thousands of rivers and enchanting lakes. And other outdoor activities such as horse riding, golf and tennis are also well catered for. In addition, there are numerous swimming pools and sport centres that offer a full range of sports

Below left. Bedroom at the Hotel Greif.
Below right. La Perla restaurant.

Stylish Places to Stay

Chic mountain lodge: Rosa Alpina Hotel & Spa. A chic spa hotel set in the craggy contours of the Dolomite Alps with mountain lodge-style rooms filled with beeswaxed wood furniture, pale marble and antique wood floors, and creamy linens; the recently refurbished St. Hubertus restaurant serves dinner in a candlelit, wood-paneled room with a blazing log fire. To warm things up further, have a lavender or rosemary-infused sauna followed by a milk or rose-petal bath for two.

Historic oasis: Hotel Greif. Situated only 300 metres from Bolzano centre makes this a fabulous location for those wanting to be in the middle of shops, restaurants and bars. The 33 individually designed rooms display modern artwork specially commissioned by different artists - the junior suite with hot tub is simply divine.

Chapel charm: Schloss Rubein. A 12th Century romantic castle, known to have been a secluded getaway for renowned singers Pavarotti and Dalla. It is surrounded by 5-hectare landscape (with swimming pool) and has spacious, decorative suites overlooking a lovely romantic courtyard.

Delicious Places to Eat

Farmhouse chic: La Perla. Fine dining restaurant with a room dedicated to an impressive wine collection. It's been painstakingly restored from an old farmhouse, but still retaining the rustic character, it's cosy and charming.

Tirolean delight: Kallmünz. Located in the center of Merano and part of Castle Kallmünz with a lovely courtyard garden. All the food served at Restaurant Kallmünz is prepared on a same-day basis, from the bread to the yogurt, from the breadsticks scented with the oregano of the Amalfi Coast to the diverse types of fresh pasta, the desserts, ice-creams and pralines.

Mountain retreat: Hermitage. The converted, authentic mountain cabin with a cosy, charming atmosphere and typical Trentino gastronomy. Situated in the Biohotel Hermitage.

Opposite page. **Top.** Stintino beach.
Bottom. Santa Teresa beach.

Adventure: Beach
Destination: Sardinia

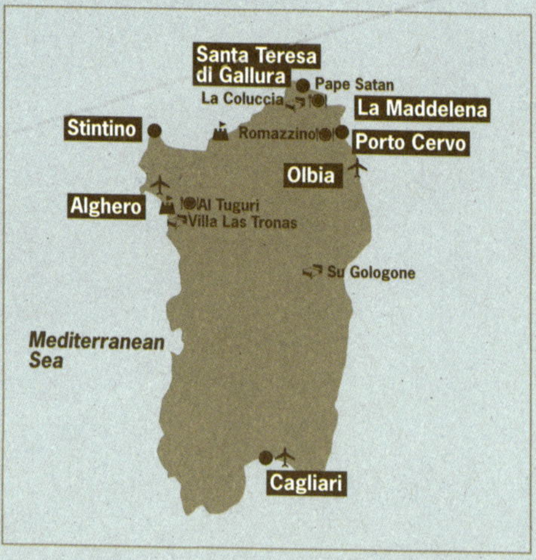

Regional Information

Small enough to be classified an island, but big enough to be a country in itself. Sardinia lies about 120 miles west of the Italian coast and bears the traces of all the civilisations that have passed through; from Carthaginian to Spanish and the extraordinary Nuraghic civilisation, whose ancient monuments lie scattered throughout the interior. Its coastline is similar to Corsica but less rugged and with incredible white sandy beaches. Its waters teem with fish and shellfish making it excellent spot for scuba divers and snorkellers, and a fabulous destination for romantic beach walks, picnics or strolls around the historical charming towns.

Sardinia's 'Emerald Coast' has long been a favourite of crowned-heads, movie stars and millionaires. The drive along the stretch of road from Olbia to Stintino is stunning, with dramatic perched hills towns and beautiful sandy beaches. There is also a little green train (known as Il Trenino Verde), which is a tourist service provided by the Sardinian Railways, and travels through scenic wildlife areas from Arbatax to Cagliari passing through the middle of the Barbagia, but only operates from June until mid September. This is a lovely experience and the elegant period coaches and fantastic railway architecture make it especially unique.

Sardinia is rich in both handicrafts and arts, its carpets, baskets, pottery and its gold filigree jewellery are both unique and of the highest quality. However if shopping is on the agenda then look no further than the designer boutiques of Porto Cervo. The most beautiful boats in Europe enter and leave this port, which is also the setting for the famous annual Rolex yacht regatta, as well as an international (and local) rich and famous holiday destination.

Opposite page. Top. La Coluccia.
Bottom. Restaurant in Porto Cervo.

Adventure: Beach **Destination:** Sardinia

The natural harbour of Santa Teresa di Gallura is home to the ferryboat that links Sardinia to Corsica and a quaint market town with sandy beaches, such as the Rena Bianca, and 10 minutes out of town sits La Marmorata. The main square in Santa Teresa is a lively spot in the summer months, with Italians holidaying and tourists dropping in and out of the port. Between Santa Teresa and Olbia lies a small port 'Palau' where you can easily catch the local 20-minute ferry to the stunning islands of La Maddalena and Caprera, where the legendary Giuseppe Garibaldi made his home, has been a National Park since 1996. The "Archipelago La Maddalena" (in Roman times known as "Cunicularìae"; rabbit islands) is made up of seven islands, and has stunning beaches, boutique shops and cafés. If you want a really special treat you can always charter a private yacht for the day and cruise around the archipelago, allowing you the freedom to stop off where you like.

Alghero is recognized to be the most Italian of all the towns (even with its Catalanic history) in Sardinia with an ancient, pretty town centre and a labyrinth network of narrow streets, churches and the nearby Grotta di Nettuno (Neptune's Grotto); a fabulous cave system carved into the cliff with long winding passages delving into the stalagmites and stalactites. Alghero is also an old fishing port with quite a lively atmosphere. The Lido is Alghero's own beach that runs all the way form Alghero to Fertilia, a small hamlet of Alghero. In the summer months the Lido comes to life with a number of bars, restaurants and pizzerias in the area, and when the sun goes down you can find live music and parties on the beach. If you don't want to be on the beach all day and want to experience a little more of the cultural side of Alghero there is the old town. Dating back to the 12th century the old town centre is truly something that must be seen to be fully appreciated. Have lunch along the battlements looking out to sea or take a stroll through the shops in the warren of cobble stone streets. As Alghero is a Catalan town much of the cuisine available is Italian there are a few Catalan influences to be found such as Paella and Catalan lobster. The rest of Sardinia offers an array of gastronomic specialities from the ancient cooking traditions of the shepherds (Suckling spit-roasted pig) to the seafood specialities of the coast.

For peace and tranquillity head towards Sintino, (the regional National Park) where there is a myriad of national parks and quite beaches perfect for a romantic picnic. "La Pelosa Beach" is the most famous and no doubt one of the most beautiful beaches in Sardinia, facing the island of Asinara with crystalline water and very fine white sand. Other beaches in the area that must be visited are; "La Pelosetta", "Le Saline", "Ezzi Mannu", and for the lovers of the rocky coastline, Capo Falcone is a must.

Stylish Places to Stay

Beachside castle: Villa Las Tronas, Alghero. Overlooking stunning and dramatic Alghero bay, this former summer residence of the Italian Royalty has been converted into a charming upmarket hotel. It's within walking distance from Alghero's old town, with shops and restaurants a plenty and romantic evening strolls on the beach.

Quiet hideaway: Hotel Su Gologone, Oliena. Decorated with colourful cushions, antiques and charm with staircases and hallways leading to gardens, terraces, quiet corners and secret hideaways – prefect for couples wanting some privacy. They also hold weddings here too, so if you haven't planned yours already, then book ahead!

Simple & chic: La Coluccia, Santa Teresa. A 'design hotel' which oozes style and glamour. Its 45 contemporary rooms are set in landscaped grounds just a few metres from its own beautiful private beach. Try the evening 'taster menu' washed down with local wine.

Delicious Places to Eat

Seafood treat: Ristorante Al Tuguri, Alghero. This is a cosy little place situated right in the heart of the old town, facing one of the typical cobbled streets of Alghero. Located in an antique dwelling in the centre of this historic Catalan town, Al Tuguri is a must-visit for all lovers of food, attracted by the skilful counterpoint between fresh inventiveness and strict tradition, that is the secret of its cuisine.

Pizza palace: Ristorante Pape Satan, Santa Teresa. Its wonderful wood fired oven produces one of the best pizza's in town and a gorgeous pretty internal courtyard. A favourite with the locals.

Gourmet delight: Romazzino. The Romazzino Restaurant in Porto Cervo on the Emerald coast in Sardinia is known for its spacious sea view terrace and exclusive innovative cuisine. Typical Sardinian cooking techniques are combined with haute cuisine giving guests a unique gourmet experience.

Opposite page. Bulgari Hotel courtyard.

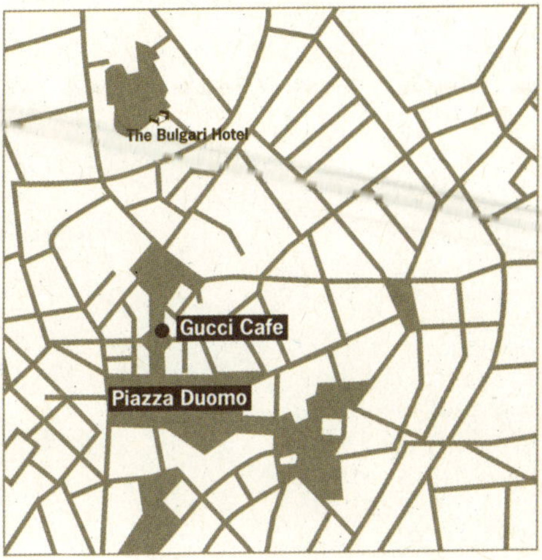

Focus On...
Shopping in Milan

Milan is either Italy's second or first city, depending on whom you ask. While Rome may be the administrative capital, Milan is the country's financial powerhouse and fashion capital. The city is vibrant and has several sights of interest, as well as being a good jumping-off place for other North Italy destinations, such as Lake Como and the Alps. It's also a good spot to spend a romantic weekend break, or as the starting point for a longer honeymoon.

In Milan, image is everything. Milan's designer clothes and furnishings are a major attraction for many fashion-conscious tourists, but not all Milan's pleasures are expensive. Sitting outside a cafe by the fantastic Duomo, admiring the well-dressed world go by; or indulging in a spot of window-shopping is enjoyable yet rather more affordable. In Milan's museums and galleries are some great works of art, while more simple pleasures include climbing up to the Duomo's roof and enjoying the tranquility and the view over the city to the mountains. The Brera and the Navigli (canal) districts are both appealing for evening strolls.

However, when it comes to shopping, Milan's main players tend to have a more enduring appeal. Prestigious showrooms and glamorous boutiques showcase designer labels from some of the world's biggest names in fashion: Gucci, Prada, Dolce & Gabbana, Armani, Fendi, Versace, Moschino – the list is endless. If you're not a shopaholic before you go, a trip to Milan may send you on your way. The new and upmarket Bulgari hotel is renowned for being a cool nightspot, designer chic heaven and its luscious spa. A perfect place for couples wanting an oasis from the city yet is central enough to explore.

Highlights

- Castello Sforzesco, paintings by da Vinci,Bellini, Titian, Van Dyck and Michelangelo.
- Il Duomo, the world's fourth-largest church and a breathtaking late-Gothic amalgamation of intricate spires and statues.
- Santa Maria delle Grazie – home to Leonardo da Vinci's famous painting, The Last Supper.
- Coffee at Gucci Caffè, in the Gucci store in Galleria Vittorio Emanuele II.
- Aperitif in Rioalto, one of Milan's most exclusive clubs.
- Dance at Hollywood Rythmoteque, Italy's most famous club (and probably the most glamorous).

Stylish Essentials

General Information

General Tourist Information
National Tourist Office
Via Marghera 2 00185
www.enit.it
T. +39 (0) 64 97 11 (info)

Tourist Information
www.italiantourism.com

Italian Tourist Information
Italian State Tourist Board
1, Princes Street
London W1B 2AY
www.italiantouristboard.co.uk/it/index.html
T. +44 (0) 20 7408 1254
F. +44 (0) 20 7399 3567
Open: Mon to Fri 9.00–17.00

Airlines

Alitalia
www.alitalia.com
T. 08714 241 424 (UK reservations)

Air France
www.airfrance.co.uk
T. 0870 142 4343 (UK reservations)

British Airways
www.ba.com
T. 0844 493 0787
(UK reservations & enquiries)

BMI
www.flybmi.com
T. 0870 6070 555
(UK reservations & enquiries)

Meridiana
www.meridiana.it
T. 0845 3555588 (UK Reservations)

Trains

Eurostar
www.eurostar.com
T. 08705 186 186 (UK bookings)

Rail Europe
For all train tickets across Europe (including TGV)
www.raileurope.co.uk

Venice

General Tourist Information
Official Online website
English & Italian
www.turismovenezia.it

Gondola Booking Contacts
San Marco
T. +39 (0) 41 522 4904
Rialto
T. +39 (0) 41 522 4904
Train Station
T. +39 (0) 41 718543

Venice Carnival Show
Teatro San Gallo, 50 metres from Piazza San Marco
www.venice-carnival-show.com
T. +39 (0) 41 241 1943
Open: Performances daily from 19.30

Palazzo Ducale (Doges Palace)
Piazza San Marco
T. +39 (0) 41 271 5911
Open: 9.00–19.00

Basilica San Marco
Piazza San Marco
T. +39 (0) 41 522 5697
Open: Mon – Sat, 9.45–17.00
Sun, 14.00–17.00

Museo Vetrario (Glass Museum)
Fondamenta Giustinian 8, Murano
T. +39 (0) 41 73 95 86
Open: Thurs – Tues, 10.00–16.00

Nove Cento
Calle del Dose,
Campo San Maurizio, San Marco
2683/84 30124 Venezia
www.novecento.biz
T. +39 (0) 41 2413765
F. +39 (0) 41 5212145

Ca Maria Adele
Dorsoduro 111 30123 Venezia
www.camariaadele.com
T. +39 (0) 41 5203078
F. +39 (0) 41 5289013

Villa Casanova
Via Orso Partecipazio, 9
30126 Venice Lido
www.casanovavenice.com
T. + 39 (0) 41 5262857
F. + 39 (0) 41 770200

Alle Testiere
Calle del Mondo Novo,
Castello 5801, Venice
T. + 39 041 5227220
Open: Tues – Sat

Ristorante Gran Caffè Quadri
Piazza San Marco 121
30124 Venice
www.quadrivenice.com
T. +39 (0) 41 5222105
Open: 9.30–23.30

Enoteca Mascareta
Calle Lunga Santa Maria Formosa,
Castello 5183;
T. +39 (0) 41 523-0744
Open: Closed Weds & Thurs,
dinner only

Dolomites

Ski Passes & Information
www.dolomitisuperski.com

Weather Forecast
www.meteotrentino.it
T. +39 (0) 461 23 89 39

Scuola di Alpinismo
Bonatical walks, climbing and glacier treks
www.catores.com
T. +39 (0) 471 798223

Trentino Music Festival
High altitude concerts from Classic, Blues and Jazz
Malghe
Summer only
T. +39 (0) 461 8390 00

Molveno's Guide Alpine Brenta Est
Rock climbing, mountaineering , guided walks for all levels
T. +39 (0) 461 586924
E. guidealpine@aptdolomitipagnella.com
Open: 8.30–22.00 July-Aug

Adrenaline Center
Head Office
"Taxi Bob", Loc. Ronco, Cabina "S"
32043 CORTINA D'AMPEZZO (BL)
T. +39 (0) 436 860808

Rosa Alpina Hotel & Spa
Strada Micura de Rü,
20 - I-39030 San Cassiano in Badia,
www.rosalpina.it
T. +39 (0) 471 849500
F. +39 (0) 471 849377

Hotel Greif
Piazza Walther Von Der Vogelweide, 1
39100 Bolzano (Trentino-Alto Adige
www.laurin.it
T. +39 (0) 471 318000

Schloss Rubein
Christomannostraße 38
I - 39012 Meran/Obermais
www.rubein.com
T. +39 (0) 473 231894
E. schloss@rubein.com

La Perla
Strada Col Alt 105
39033 Corvara Alta Badia Dolomiti
T. +39 (0) 471 831000

Kallmunz
Sandplatz/Piazza Rena, 12
39012 Merano (Bolzano)
www.kallmuenz.it
T. +39 (0) 473 212917
E. info@kallmuenz.it
F. +39 (0) 473 239802

Stube Hermitage
Via Castelletto Inferiore, 69
38084 Madonna di Campiglio (Trento)
www.stubehermitage.it
T. +39 (0) 465 441558
E. info@biohotelhermitage.it
F. +39 (0) 465 441618

Sardinia

Yacht Charter in Sardinia
Tours La Maddalena, Paula, Porto Cervo and Cala di Volpe
http://barracuda-yacht-charter.com
T. +44 (0)1273 422373
(UK Company)

Moby Line Ferries
Ferries Operating year-round to Sardinia
Book Tickets online
www.mobylines.it

Sardinia Green train
Italian Only Site – Good maps & Routes
www.treninoverde.com

Scuba Diving Information
www.scubatravel.co.uk/italy/

Grotta di Nettuno
T. +39 (0)79 979054
Open: 9.00–19.00 Apr-Sept
10.00–14.00 Nov-March

Villa Las Tronas
Lungomare Valencia, 1
07041, Alghero, Sardinia
www.hotelvillalastronas.com
T. +39 (0) 79 981 818
F. +39 (0) 79 981 044

La Coluccia
Località Conca Verde
07028 Santa Teresa Gallura, Sardinia
www.designhotels.com/lacoluccia
T. 0800 37 46 83 57
(UK reservations)

Hotel Su Gologone
Localitat Su Gologone
08025 Oliena, Sardinia
www.hotelsugologone.com
T. +39 (0) 784 287 512

Ristorante Al Tuguri
Al Tuguri
113 Via Maiorca
Alghero (Sassari)
T. +39 (0) 79 976 772

Ristorante Pape Satan
Santa Teresa di Gallura
Via del Mare 36
T. +39 (0) 789 754600

Romazzino
Costa Smeralda
07020 Porto Cervo (Sassari)
www.hotelromazzino.it
T. +39 (0) 789 977111

Milan

Bvlgari Hotel Milan
Via Privata Fratelli Gabba 7/b
20121 Milano
www.bulgarihotels.com
T. +39 (0) 2 805 8051

Fidenze Village Shopping
Via San Michele Campagna, Fidenza
www.fidenzavillage.com
T. +39 (0) 524 33551

Kasbah Tamadot. Courtesy of Virgin Ltd.

MOROCCO

Marrakesh | Essaouira | Fès | Atlas Mountains |

MOROCCO

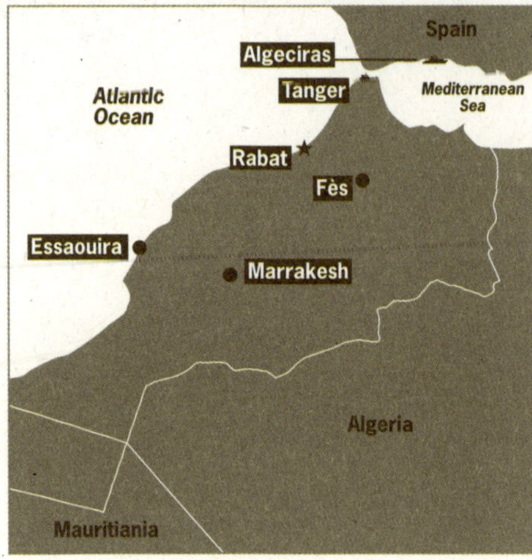

Why is this place so special?

Morocco is an exotic, enchanting country and located just 3 hours from the UK meaning it is accessible even for a weekend honeymoon, yet it is also special, seductive and timeless. It never ceases to amaze and charm visitors who experience its beautiful and varied landscapes, from the Atlas Mountains, to the stunning sunsets of Essaouira and the enigmatic ancient city of Marrakesh. Spending a weekend in a luxury 'riad' in Marrakesh or Fès, or stretching your muscles shopping in some of the colourful outdoor markets, or indulging in some off-piste desert driving over sugar-soft dunes are just some of the highlights.

It has often been said that the people are the pulse of a nation; this is certainly true of Morocco. The rich culture and diversity is reflected in every inch of the vibrant nation that trade frantically and enthusiastically in the bustling streets. The locals have a long and fascinating heritage, though they've slowly started to embrace the modernizing of their world. You'll still find donkeys, pulling carts and carrying all kinds of merchandise, watermen in colourful attire and every so often you'll see relics and hand-carved doorways stemming from medieval times.

Gastronomic indulgence is also one of Morocco's highlights. Moroccan cuisine has long been considered as one of the most diversified cuisines in the world, and locally (as with many places) dining is very much at the heart of socializing with family and friends. The mixed cuisine is a result of the centuries-long interaction of Morocco with the outside world. The cuisine of Morocco is a mix of Berber, Spanish, Corsican, Portuguese, Moorish, Middle Eastern, Mediterranean, and African. Herbs and spices such as saffron and mint are used extensively in famous dishes such as Tajine or Harira and mint tea and dates are usually served along with smoking a flavoured shisha (known as a hookah or waterpipe). The smells, sounds and colours make Morocco a magnificent treat for those who love satisfying their senses.

Top. The Kasbah, Morocco. **Bottom.** Leather dyeing, Morocco.

Couples who enjoy a few pampered treats you won't have to look far to experience a traditional 'hammam' (a real institution in Morocco) a body exfoliation, ghasoul wrap or a simple full-body massage. Several destinations such as Marrakesh, Essaouira and Fès are quickly becoming recognized as "well-being" destinations, with Essaouira focusing more on seawater therapy due to its location on the Atlantic Ocean. Morocco is an ideal place to get away from it all and relax as well as absorb some local culture and absorb the natural beauty.

Fast Facts

Capital: Rabat.

Location: Morocco has international borders with Algeria to the East, Spain to the North and a coast on the Atlantic Ocean that reaches past the Strait of Gibraltar into the Mediterranean Sea.

Population: 33,700,000.

Religion: Muslim 98.7%, Christian 1.1% and Jewish 0.2%.

Languages: Official language is Arabic but French is widely spoken.

Opposite page. From top. Homme de Mekhnes, Terrace overlooking Fès, Djemaa el Fna.

Getting there and exploring around

With international airports in Marrakesh and Fès, Morocco is well linked to Europe, Africa and the Middle East. Driving to Morocco is also a possibility and reasonably straightforward. There are a variety of car ferries and jetfoils operating between Algericas in Spain and Morocco's Tangier and Ceuta. There are also ferry trips twice a week from Gibraltar to Tangier.

Morocco's Office National des Chemins de Fer (ONCF) operates one of the most modern rail and bus systems in Africa, linking most of the main centres. The trains are generally comfortable, fast and a better option than the buses - if only because sleeping cars are available for many overnight trips. Lines go as far south as Marrakesh. If you miss the train, the buses are by no means a last-ditch option, the bus network is dense and efficient in most areas. Running alongside the bus services are shared taxis. These are the workhorses of the Moroccan road - normally outdated Mercedes vehicles which you'll see belting along the highways or gathered in great flocks near bus stations.

Shared taxis are a big feature of Morocco's public transport system and link towns to their nearest neighbours in a kind of 'leapfrogging' system, going from one town to another, en route to a final destination. The fixed-rate fares are higher than bus fares. Renting a car isn't cheap in Morocco, but deals can be struck with the smaller agencies. Petrol (gas) is available pretty much everywhere. There are police checks on most main roads in Morocco but these rarely affect foreigners.

The bigger cities have public bus services. Petits taxis are a common sight in most cities and major towns, they're licensed to carry up to three passengers and can be a useful way to avoid heat exhaustion and/or hustlers.

Best time of year to visit

Generally the climate in Morocco remains quite dry for most of the year although a little rain can be expected between November and March.

The temperature can be incredibly high in the Southern and South-eastern desert areas, but the temperature drops considerably in the higher lying mountainous areas, even getting to freezing point at night – so warmer clothing is a must.

July and August, the hottest months and can be wonderful on the coast. Spring, which comes late by European standards (around April to May), is perhaps the best overall time to visit. During this time Morocco experiences a warm summer climate in the South and in the mountains as well as on the Mediterranean and Atlantic coasts.

? Must know before you go

Kindly decline. You may be inundated with offers and deals in the souks, it would be wise to avoid being rude or aggressive. If you are genuinely not interested in making any purchases, a friendly decline and your body language will likely tell them this. In general, never keep silent if you are offered something, it is considered to be rude and offensive.

Tour guides. You will often find yourself confronted by numerous tour guides in the bigger cities. Some of these are official and can really enhance your trip. Many more, however, are unofficial. Be cautious and ask the hotel for a recommendation if you are unsure.

Codes of dress. Legs and shoulders are considered to be 'private body parts' and men and woman should do their utmost to keep these areas covered. Respect these codes especially in the main 'medina'.

Highlights

The souks. During the summer season temperatures pass 40°C for months. The coolness of the stone houses makes the souks a place to hide from the sun and an excellent place to observe local life.

Shisha fun. Smoke an 'apple' infused Shisha (known as a Hookah or Waterpipe) and relax with a fresh 'Mint Tea' and sticky Medjool dates in Djemma el-Fna, the heart of Marrakesh.

Be entertained. Djemaa el-Fna owes most of its fame to the large number of spectacles going on all the time. Snake charmers, singers, storytellers, healers and fakirs attract a dominantly Moroccan audience.

Relax on a beach. Head to Essouria for wild, stunning beaches and a breath of fresh air.

Tip for the Trip

"Avoid hanging the 'Please Clean Room' tag on your door. It's an obvious sign you are not in and leaves you susceptible to theft."

Carlo

Opposite page. Top. Spices in a souk.
Bottom. Marrakesh medina.

Adventure: Gastronomy
Destination: Marrakesh

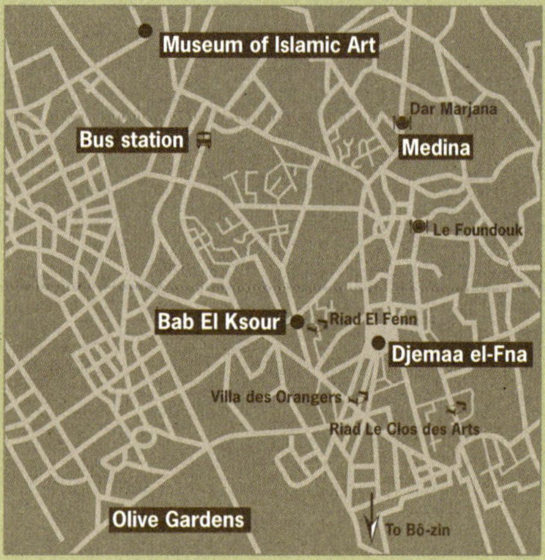

Regional Information

Marrakesh is very much the destination of the moment; it's a city of drama and its spectacular backdrop of the Atlas Mountains makes this also an incredible setting. Marrakesh is also Morocco's second largest city and as its population continues to rise, so has its tourism. It has a prosperous industrial area and is the most significant market and organizational centre of Southern Morocco. Marrakesh does not have many historical monuments and buildings; its beauty lies in the atmosphere and spectacular location. It's a perfect place to start a honeymoon and staying in one of the luxury riads and being pampered can be a romantic treat – or alternatively use it as a stop-over point before exploring the country further. Although it is not essential to have a tour guide in Marrakesh as a good map will guide you perfectly, sometimes it pays when you are visiting areas outside the city.

The mysterious 'riads' with sheltered courtyards and scattered floor cushions, behind ornate doors are wonderfully charming and seductive places to stay. The souks (markets) are a labyrinth where you can lose yourself (and your cash) haggling for gold, spices, kaftans and hand-made carpets. Although during the sweltering summer there are hordes of tourists, there is plenty of atmosphere due to the Marrakesh Arts festival (held in July), pilgrimage and feasts. It's also a great place to observe the locals in their daily life.

CAYENNE
TAGINE
CURRY
PILI PILI
SAFRAN
CORIANDRE
PIMENT
COUSCOUS
INGWER
MASSIS
CLOU DE GIROFLE NELKEN
NOIX DE MOSCADE
CANNELLE
CHILLI
PAPRIKA
THYM
LAVANDE
POIVRE-BLANC WEISSER PFEFFER
ROSMARIN
CANNELLE ZIMT
KINZING
SAFRAN
ORIGON
PILI-PILI
EUCALIPTUS RHUM SCHNUPFEN
TAGINE MÉLANGE
ROMARIN
EUCALIPTUS SCHNUP

Adventure: Gastronomy
Destination: Marrakesh

The souks are interesting places in alleys and small squares that are dedicated to specific crafts and it is here that you can often watch part of the making process. There are a number of souks worth visiting and you can easily find the way to the souks on your own. Even if you get a little lost, you will find that this is part of the fun. The most appealing times to visit the souks are early morning and late afternoon when they auction off merchandise to the public. The best souks to visit are Souk Rahba Qdima for tapestries, carpets, rugs and Souk des Teinturiers, which is an ancient tannery, remained unchanged for hundreds of years. Finally, Souk el Attarine for perfumes and fragrant oils.

Djemaa el-Fna is the main square at the heart of old Marrakesh and as night falls is full of activity – from alfresco food bazaar, street theatre to snake charmers and hookah (shisha) cafés. Henna tattooists are always on hand to paint your hands and feet with traditional designs. Be drawn back into a frenzied world where jugglers and storytellers jostle for position with snake charmers, magicians and acrobats. Your nose will guide you to row upon row of open-air food stalls, whose pungent smoke fill the air with mouth-watering aromas. Just wandering through this area is a pure delight.

The Marrakesh Museum is also a place worth visiting; it houses exhibitions of Moroccan art and sculpture, both traditional and contemporary. There is also a small bookshop and café in the entrance courtyard. With the summers in Marrakesh being so hot nobody seems to want to do much, a perfect place to do nothing is in the gardens, with many picnic spots, lake-sized pools and cool and quiet surroundings.

Marrakesh eating and drinking options are abundant. The Medina is where you'll find most of the city's French-style cafés, bistros and restaurants and virtually all the bars. There's plenty of choice for meals, including the spectacle of the Djemaa el-Fna food stalls, many inexpensive café-restaurants and a number of up-market palace-restaurants offer traditional Moroccan cuisine at its very best. For those who like experimenting with spices, there are several 'cookery workshops' for anyone wanting to discover the pleasures of Moroccan cooking. Workshops are often conducted by a 'dada' (a traditional Moroccan chef) and organized in small groups, making it pretty personal and fun, especially for couples.

Below from left. Bedroom at the Villa des Orangers. Le Foundouk.

Stylish Places to Stay

Deluxe delight: Villa des Orangers. A luxury five-star riad at the edge of the Medina with elegant, hand-carved wooden furniture and a stunning courtyard with a roof terrace and plunge pool. Perfect for relaxing after a long day in the Souks. Many things make this place stand out from the crowd as a place to stay, non more so than its attention to detail. Sumptuous rooms and a beautiful swimming pool ideal to cool off in.

Rooftop fun: Riad El Fenn. Wake up to fresh pastries and coffee at this oasis. Located near 'Bab El ksour' this large riad town-house is a perfect spot for sundown drinks on the rooftop terrace, overlooking the medina and the atlas mountains.

Modern Morocco: Riad Le Clos des Arts. A quaint authentic riad located a short walk from Djamaa el-fna and the Bahia Palace with a modern Moroccan twist. It's very small and popular with only 4 suites and 2 rooms so the service is personal and friendly, but you need to book far in advance. This lovely riad is located only 5 minutes from he main square and has an amazing rooftop terrace to wind down after a hard days bartering in the souks.

Delicious Places to Eat

Typical Moroccan: Dar Marjana. The setting is worth a thousand words...located near the palace gates in the medina, this restaurant provides a true Moroccan experience. The dining area overlooks the private courtyard and fountain and decoration is extravagant with brocade divans. Local music is played by Gnaouas and Moroccan wine is served. It's popular so reservations are recommended.

Cutting-edge chic: Le Foundouk. A new-styled chic restaurant providing an intimate setting for special evening meals. The food is a Tunisian and Moroccan mix with a French and Italian twist. Book ahead on weekends as its gets very busy.

Fun & glamorous: Bô-zin. A short taxi ride away from the town, dine on a fusion of Moroccan, Thai and Mediterranean dishes on the palm-studded terrace. They have a chill-out area outside where you can relax after dinner. Saturdays are livelier with a DJ spinning tunes.

Oppostie page. Top. Essaouira Beach, Courtesy of Dreamstime. **Bottom.** L'Heure Bleue Palais & Spa.

Adventure: Beach
Destination: Essaouira

Regional Information

Essaouira is located in the Southwest region of Morocco, and is a grand escape from the more tourist-centered beaches of Agadir and generally popular with independent travellers (only rarely do you see package tours here). It's a small, enchanting coastal city only a two-hour drive from Marrakesh, the locals call it "plages sauvages" or wild beaches. Unspoilt, sandy beaches thickly fringed by argan trees, (which are found only in Morocco) and small white and blue houses give to this quaint fishing port a very romantic atmosphere. Its original name was Tassort, which refers to its Kasbah, fortress-like walls. Its name is derived from Tashelhit, the Southern, Souss Berber language. In Moroccan Arabic, it's called Saouira, which literally means 'picture'.

This relaxed, hippie and wind-surfers' paradise is just that – picture perfect. It is one reason that Orson Wells chose to shoot scenes for Shakespeare's Othello on its coast. Essaouira has attracted foreign visitors, expats, and artists for decades. Allegedly Jimmy Hendrix was attracted to its mystical qualities when he hung out and even tried purchasing the entire nearby village of Diabat. Therein, the muse of the French or Portuguese ruins led him to write his song, "Castles in the Sand". White sand beaches stretch as far as you can see (covering more than 10km up to Sim Cap) and water sport lovers from all over the world return to these beaches each year, surfers appreciate the huge waves and scuba divers enjoy the clear waters. The white sand beaches are magnificent and ideal for romantic walks or running, though, unfortunately, they are not great for swimming due to strong currents and waves.

Adventure: Beach
Destination: Essaouira

Dating back 3,000 years, Essaouira is a fortified fishing village which has played a very important role throughout Moroccan history, at one point controlled by the Portuguese, then the French, before control was returned to the Kingdom of Morocco in 1956. The Portuguese influence is marked by the incredible architecture and its light brown stone. A good example of this can be seen when you enter into the city's main portals. Awe-inspiring Arabic calligraphy adorns the centerpiece and reads "baraka," which literally means "divine attention". UNESCO has also given the city a lot of attention and has funded the painstakingly careful task of restoring its walls, ramparts, and Catholic Church.

Essaouira is also famous throughout Morocco for the artisana products, there are numerous workshops hidden in the tiny and winding passageways of the ancient medina where you can watch artists using age old methods. Workshops of wood carving and marquetry are located along the Rue de Skala. Local wood called thuya is used in the unique artisanal products. Thuya resembles mahogany and is becoming scarce in the region, making it a good investment piece.

The Pottery Quarter is situated on Safi hill and at almost any time of day you will find dozens of potters working. Local clay is used for the pottery and is quite chalky and very rich in iron oxide. The soaking, drying and kneading of the clay makes the process rather lengthy, and visitors are welcome to watch as long as they wish.

Essaouira is undoubtedly the most relaxed city in Morocco, which is perfect for a 'get away from it all' type honeymooner. However, the fisherman's port does come to life when the boats return from a long day at sea. The fish auctions are great to watch and if you enjoy seafood you have come to the right place. Most of the local restaurants have daily fresh fish specials which represent good value for money and excellent quality.

Below from top. L'heure Bleue Palais & Spa. L'heure Bleue Palais pool. L'heure Bleue Palais Restaurant.

Stylish Places to Stay

Luxury elegance: L'heure Bleue Palais & Spa. Incredibly elegantly designed with excellent service and is a total oasis of calm in Essaouira's medina. The spa is also a wonderful retreat.

Town setting: Riad O Marine. O Marine is a fresh gem in the heart of Essaouira. They serve breakfast on the roof top terrace with views over the town, a real highlight.

Beach chic: Madada Mogador. Wonderful interior design, a location to die for within the ramparts of beautiful old Essaouira and the azure seas of Morocco in abundant view, all help make the Madada Mogador a rather special place to stay.

Delicious Places to Eat

Patio chic: Dar Loubane. Dating back to the 18th century this riad is beautifully decorated. You can dine on the patio lit up by candelabras or in one of the interior dining rooms depending on your mood. Gnaoua musicians usually provide entertainment on Saturday evenings. They accept credit cards.

Local charm: Le Patio. Laid out on a charming patio surrounded by alcoves that can be transformed into small private rooms, this restaurant is the ideal place for a young and festive clientele. At the bar, you will meet Antoine and Marie, the owners, who moved from Besançon in France to open this restaurant four years ago. The menu has a daily selection of fish dishes, depending on the catch. You may order up until 11 pm.

Splendid & special: L'Heure Bleue Palais Restaurant. This Relais & Châteaux listed palace was once the home of an Arab chief. It has been remarkably restored, preserving all of its past elegance. There is a large, shady patio and sophisticated décor incorporating different cultures and a beautiful roof-top pool, where you can also take your meals.

Opposite page. **Clockwise from top left.** Typical Moroccan local. Images of Fès medina.

Adventure: Culture + Art
Destination: Fès

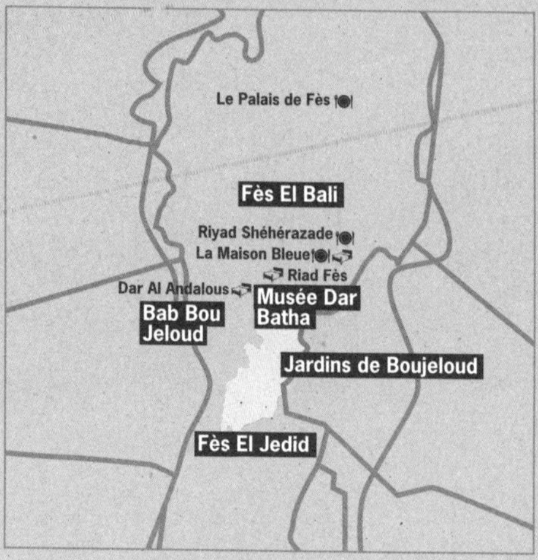

Regional Information

Getting the most out of Fès is easy; the difficult part is leaving. Fès is the former capital of Morocco and one of the oldest and largest medieval cities in the world and a wonderful location for those who enjoy culture, art and history, and plenty to keep you busy for three or four days.

The great novelist Amin Maalouf writes of uncovering Fès' layers "veil by veil, like a bride in her marriage chamber", and though most visitors resemble bashful bridegrooms on their first day in town, they're usually pretty swift to get into the connubial swing of things here.

English travel writer Nina Epton describes Fès, the oldest of the four imperial cities, in this romantic way; "Fès is ancient and noble, a voluptuous and subtle charmer, overpowering the soul, lulling one's senses with the poison. Here there is no sense of time and space. Here magic carpets are woven, love filters are brewed... No one can spend a night during Ramadan under the moonlight ramparts of Fès, submitted to the aphrodisiacal influence of Arab music, and still remain entirely European." Ramadan is the Muslim festival of fasting and is the most important event in the Islamic Calendar which is celebrated by Muslims all over the world. The arrival of the crescent moon in the night sky signals the start of 30 days of fasting during which Muslims don't eat, drink or smoke during the day, eating all their meals before sunrise and after sunset. Consequently, many of Morocco's cafes and coffee shops throng with activity each evening during Ramadan. Fasting is one of the pillars of the Islamic faith and reminds Muslims of the plight of the poor, sick and needy. Eid al-Fitr marks the end of the 30-day fasting period and is a great celebration throughout the Muslim world. This is a great time of year to visit and to experience this event.

Opposite page. Left. Deluxe room at the Riad Fès. **Right.** Riyad Shéhérazade.

Adventure: Culture + Art
Destination: Fès

Called the Athens of North Africa, Fès is the intellectual, religious and artistic capital of Morocco. Life has a distinctively medieval flavour in this city and the medina with its mosques, bazaars, narrow streets, can also boast the best artisans in the country. If you like to bargain, this is the place to sharpen your skills since the Moroccans excel in this art. Shopping in the open markets with the aromas of incense and spices, among all kind of exotic merchandise is an unforgettable experience. The Fès medina is famous for its merchants, its artists and talented craftsmen still carrying on the trade traditions. Its many quarters are specialized by guilds, and the crafts industry is the driving force behind the old city. Among the special crafts Fès is famous for: fine woodcarving, brassware, silks, pottery, leather goods and bookbinding. Andalusian music, Berber songs and dances are equally appreciated. The medina is best explored on foot (although you can get guided tours) it's best to navigate your own way round, preferably during the daylight hours if you are a little nervous.

The Boujeloud Gardens (Jardins de Boujeloud) is a real haven with an open air cafe and many picnic spots. The Jardins de Boujeloud are situated between Fès El Jedid and Fès El Bali, near the Vieux Méchouar. They are bordered by the Avenue des Francais and the Rue de l'Unesco. It's just within a stone's throw of the Dar Batha Museum. A good walk around the city can start here, through the Royal Palace and old town end at the Fès El Jedid a 13th-century city enclosed with separate set of fortifications.

Music lovers will enjoy the annual 'Fès Festival of World Sacred Music' which takes place usually in June. Fès has become a global music destination since the start of the festival following the first Gulf War and the festival lures both musicians seeking fresh ideas and renewed inspiration as well as international music lovers, many of whom return year after year. VIP guests last year included members of the Irish supergroup U2, composer Osvaldo Golijov, and Queen Rania of Jordan.

The historical city of Meknès located 60 km from Fès in the fertile plain of Saïss, is protected by the Rif and Middle Atlas Mountains. In the sixteen hundreds it was the imperial city of sultan Moulay Ismail, a close friend of France's Louis XIV. They shared the same passion for building and grandeur. The sultan turned it into a impressive city in Spanish-Moorish style, surrounded by high walls with great doors, where the harmonious blending of the Islamic and European styles of the 17th century Maghreb are still evident today. Meknès is certainly less touristy than some of the other Moroccan cities; it can be visited in a day trip and is a great place for exploration of Morocco's finest mosques and medina's without getting hassled by the locals.

Stylish Places to Stay

Delux delight: Riad Fès. A wonderful combination of Moroccan architecture and contemporary style, Riad Fes is located in the most popular part of the medina, a few minutes away from the Blue Gate.

Moroccan style: Riad Maison Bleue. Riad Maison Bleue is absolutely delightful, with superior service in every respect. Rooms are very large and authentically Moroccan. Many creative and artistic touches, plus funny little twisting staircases leading to fantasy hideaway rooms and terraces.

Palace for a princess: Dar al Andalous. This gorgeous place is tucked away towards the end of Rue Derb Bennani Douh and comprises of two connecting houses that have been reconstructed into one fabulous building. The imposing large wooden door opens onto candlelit hallways that lead to the central hall. It is like a little palace inside with no attention to detail spared.

Delicious Places to Eat

Local delight: Le Palais de Fès. The Palais de Fès, a sumptuous abode, run according to Fassie family traditions is an exceptional place from both an architectural and gastronomic point of view. The quality of the cuisine is undeniable.

Private retreat: La Maison Bleue. Built in 1915, this exquisite residence still bears the mark of its first and eminent owner, Mohammed El Abbadi, astrologer, man of law and professor at the University of Qaraouiyine. His library remains and bears witness to the culture and knowledge that prevailed in this dwelling. The dishes are prepared according to the purest traditions. The cuisine is subtle and elegant, and is a worthy match for this privileged venue.

Ambiance & charm: Riyad Shéhérazade. The Riad Sheherazade is a 19th century marvel, where your dreams of a thousand and one nights come true. Its sumptuous rooms and suites perfectly combine sobriety and sheer luxury. This venue is one of the capitals of Moroccan cuisine, respectful of tradition, but also refined and inventive. A delightful setting with lively music and lovely ambiance.

Opposite page. View of the Atlas Mountains from Kasbah Tamadot, Courtesy of Virgin.

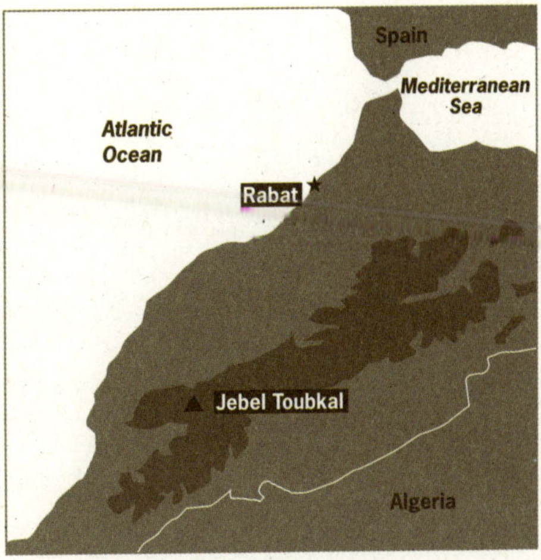

Focus On...
Atlas Mountains

Morocco's varied geography includes no less than four separate mountain ranges, in addition to lush river valleys, beautiful sandy coasts, and wide expanses of desert. The three most prominent mountain ranges, which run parallel to each other from the southwest to the northeast, are the Middle Atlas, the High Atlas, and the Anti-Atlas. The ascent of the country's highest peak, Jebel Toukbal (13,665 ft./4,165 metres), is a spectacular and not particularly difficult High Atlas trek. The Atlas Mountains near Marrakesh are also home to hundreds of small villages inhabited by the Berber people, the indigenous population of Morocco. Berber Adventures offers single and multi-day trips from Marrakesh to small villages in the High Atlas region. Travellers can experience Berber life and culture firsthand, visiting Berber homes and encountering the people face-to-face. To understand Moroccan culture in its entirety, these cultural excursions are a must.

If you want to climb the mountains there are plenty of self-guided trekking companies, which can help you with a map and a mule to carry your bags, or there are plenty of tailor-made trekking holiday companies who can arrange everything including a local Berber guide and accommodation.

Alternatively you can stay near the Atlas Mountains at Richard Branson's rural luxury retreat 'Kasbah Tamadot'. A stunning and exclusive hideaway near Asni, perched dramatically on a hilltop and surrounded by the peaks of the High Atlas. Kasbah Tamadot has compiled an array of 1 to 5-day guided excursions, ranging from a gentle wander through the nearby Ourika valley to a fully-fledged hike or 4x4 trips across the desert. They can also organise hot air balloon rides and breakfast with the local Berbers.

Stylish Essentials

General Information

Moroccan National Tourist Office in the UK
205 Regent Street, 2nd Floor,
London W1B 4HB, UK
www.visitmorocco.org
T. 020 7437 0073

Airlines

Air France
www.airfrance.co.uk
T. 0870 142 4343 (UK reservations)

British Airways
www.ba.com
T. 0844 493 0 787
(UK reservations & enquiries)

BMI
T. 0870 6070 555 (UK reservations & enquiries)
www.flybmi.com

Trains

Rail Europe
For all train tickets across Europe (including TGV)
www.raileurope.co.uk

Ferry

Trasmediterranea
From Algeciras to Tanger
www.trasmediterranea.es

Marrakesh

Marrakesh Arts festival
Fondation Festival Marrakech - Théâtre Royal
www.marrakechfestival.com
T. +212 (0) 24 43 20 21
F. +212 (0) 24 43 97 77
14th – 19th July

Cookery Classes
La Maison Arabe
1, Derb Assehbe
Bab Doukkala
Marrakesh
www.lamaisonarabe.com
T. +212 (0) 24 38 70 10
F. + 212 (0) 24 38 72 21

Riad Le Clos des Arts
50 Derb T'Bib Riad Zitoun J'Did
Marrakesh
www.lcclosdesarts.com
T. +212 (0) 24 37 51 59

Villa des Orangers
6, Rue Sidi Mimoun
Place Ben Tachfine
Marrakesh
www.villadesorangers.com
T. +212 (0) 24 38 46 38

Riad El Fenn
Derb Moullay Abdullah Ben Hezzian
Bab El Ksour
Marrakesh
www.riadelfenn.com
T. +212 (0) 24 44 12 10

Dar Marjana
15, Derb Sidi Ali Tair Bab Doukkala
Marrakesh
www.darmarjanamarrakech.com
T. +212 (0) 44 38 51 10
Open: Evenings only

Le Foundouk
55, Souk Hal Fassi,
Kay Bennahid,
Marrakech
www.foundouk.com
T. +21 (0) 24 37 81 90
Open: Lunch & dinner, closed Mondays

Bô-zin
Dour Lahna
Route de l'Ourika
www.bo-zin.com
T. +212 (0) 24 38 80 12
Open: Daily from 8pm

Essaouira

Madada Mogador
5, rue Youssef el fassi
44000 Essaouira
www.madada.com
T. +212 (0) 24 47 55 12

Riad O Marine
T. +212 (0) 24 43 15 37 (Head Office)
www.riadlotus.com

L'heure Bleue Palais & Spa
2, rue Ibn Batouta
44100 Essaouira
www.relaischateaux.com
T. + 212 (0) 24 78 34 34

Dar Loubane
24, rue du Rif
Essaouira
T. +212 (0) 44 47 62 96

Le Patio
28 bis, rue Moulay Rachid
Essaouira
T. +212 (0) 24 47 41 66

L'Heure Bleue Palais Restaurant
2, rue Ibn Batouta
44100 Essaouira
T. +212 (0) 24 78 34 34
Open: Lunch & Dinner

Fès

Fès Tourist Office
Place de la Resistance
Fès
Morocco

Fès Festival
Fondation Esprit de Fès
Sidi Al Khayat, BP 629
Fès, 30200 Maroc
www.fesfestival.com
T. +212 (0) 35 74 05 35
E. festivaldefes@fesfestival.com

Jardins de Boujeloud
Fès El Djedid
Open: 9.00–18.00

Riad Fès
Derb Ben Slimane,
Zerbtana
Fès
www.riadfes.com
T. +212 (0) 35 94 76 10

Dar al Andalous
14, Derb Bennani, Douh
Quartier Batha,
Fès
www.dar-alandalous.com
T. +212 (0) 35 74 07 00

Riad Maison Bleue
33 Derb el mitter
Talaa el Kabira
Fès
www.maisonbleue.com
T. +212 (0) 35 74 18 73

Atlas Mountains

Kasbah Tamadot
BP 67
042150 Asni
Marrakesh
www.kasbahtamadot.virgin.com
T. +212 (0) 24 36 82 00

Berber Adventures
BP 9653, Marrakech Medina, 40008
info@berberadventures.com
www.berberadventures.com
T. +212 (0) 7237 26 68
E. info@berberadventures.com

Sherpa Expeditions
Walking in Atlas Mountains
www.sherpa-walking-holidays.co.uk

Terrace room in the Uma Ubud.

INDONESIA

Java | Bali | Lombok | Komodo National Park

INDONESIA

Why is this place so special?

The name Indonesia has its roots in two Greek words: 'Indos' meaning Indian and 'Nesos' which means islands. It is an appropriate description of the archipelago as there are estimated to be a staggering 17,508 islands. Five main islands and thirty smaller archipelagos are home to the majority of the population, these being Sumatra, Kalimantan, Sulawesi, Irian Jaya and last but not least Java, home to about 70% of the country's population. Whilst the main five islands may be home to the majority, many travellers gravitate towards the pristine beaches of Lombok; explore the museums in Java or indulge in a spa treatment in Bali.

Bali is an island of overwhelming beauty. Its hillsides are covered with rice paddies, its interiors are tropical, its beaches magical and the spas are world class. Java is a long and narrow island, with a string of volcanic mountains along its backbone. It is the political, economic and geographical centre of Indonesia, with a blend of historic and cultural influences which date back many centuries. Lombok is dominated by spectacular Mount Rinjani, and features many tranquil beaches and countryside. The island is home to a lively cultural scene, which has both Sasak and Balinese influences.

Like the people on Indonesia's many islands, Indonesia's culture is a wonderful mix. It is a tapestry reflected by the 300 separate ethnic groups, which is clearly expressed by the varied (and intricate) architecture, temple ceremonies, dance, prayers and spiritual offerings of food and flowers, and ornate Buddhist monuments. Wedding ceremonies also have their own uniqueness, respectively revealing the philosophy of marriage as an important part of human life – visitors may be lucky enough to be invited to an Indonesian wedding, which is usually a colourful, atmospheric and pretty lively affair. However, it is the locals who really set this destination apart – charming, warm and friendly and genuine; which makes it a pleasure for everyone visiting.

From top. Volcano, Losari Coffee Plantation, Java. Coffee scrub treatment, Losari Coffee Plantation, Java. Traditional Java gate.

Indonesia is an exceptional honeymoon destination for those looking to escape from the typical 'resort' scene, as local daily life is aplenty as are locally run boutique guesthouses with plenty of charm and character. It also makes for an excellent spot, if you are intending on travelling to other parts of Asia, such as Thailand or Australia as flight connections are direct, inexpensive and frequent. Whilst travelling to Indonesia from the UK may take time (and money) to reach, accommodation bargains can be found, similarly restaurants and excursions can be good value for money.

Fast Facts

Capital: Jakarta.

Location: Located in South East Asia comprising of 17,508 islands. The country shares land borders with Papua New Guinea, East Timor and Malaysia.

Population: 234,693,997.

Religion: 86.1% Muslim, 5.7% Protestant, 3% Catholic, 1.8% Hindu, 3.4% other.

Languages: Official language is Bahasa Indonesia which is akin to Malay, although there are around 300 distinct native ethnicities and about 580 different languages and dialects.

Opposite page. From top. Indonesian doorway. The Borobudar Temple, Java. Yoga sunrise on the Borobudar Temple, Java.

Getting there and exploring around

Most travellers arrive by air, either directly or via Jakarta, although island hoppers (with more time to spare) can catch a ferry from Singapore (via Batam) to Java or Sumatra. There are frequent direct flights to Jakarta and Denpasar (Bali) from major airline hubs across Asia such as Singapore, Bangkok and Hong Kong and there are direct flights from major Australian cities too. If visiting Australia for example Bali is only a 5 hour flight from Sydney, so it maybe worth the hop over if you are in the region.

Getting around Indonesia is pretty simple. Bali has direct domestic flights which connect Java, Lombok and Surabaya (Java) and outlying islands on a daily basis. The most reliable are Merpati and Silk Air. Although fares have increased considerably in recent years they are still pretty good value.

A public ferry shuttles constantly between the Western Balinese port of Gilimanuk and Ketapang in Eastern Java and also between Lembar in Lombok and Padangbai in Bali (the crossing takes about 4-8 hours). Bounty Cruises also offer private executive class ferry trips between Benoa (Bali) and Lombok (via Nusa Lembongan) and takes less time (2 hrs 45 mins) and is more comfortable.

Although hiring a car isn't particularly recommended (the roads in Bali can be hazardous) tourist shuttle buses, running between the major tourist centres are comfortable and convenient.

Best time of year to visit

Although it is hot and humid all year round, Indonesia has two basic seasons: rainy and dry. The dry season from April to October is the best time to visit as some activities and road travel can be difficult during the rainy season. This is also when most of the festivals take place (i.e. Bali Arts Festival in June/July).

The rainy season (also when tropical monsoons can hit) runs from October to April with Ramadam occurring in November/December, and it can be sometimes difficult for non-Muslim travellers to eat and drink during daylight hours. However, the end of the month-long fast there are public holidays and impressive celebrations.

Temperatures along the coast tend to be higher at around 30C (88F), while inland and highland areas are cooler, particularly at night. So warmer clothing is generally needed.

? Must know before you go

Footwear etiquette. Shoes must always be removed when entering a place of worship, home, hotel room or spa. Leave your shoes outside as a mark of respect and to keep living areas clean.

Using your hands. Use your right hand in giving or receiving any items, including money. In Indonesia, the left-hand is considered dirty and if extended to another person, this may be perceived as an insult. Pointing with your index finger or beckoning people towards you is extremely impolite. Do not touch adults or children on the head (especially in Bali) nor point to anything with your foot as both these gestures will take great offense.

Helping those less fortunate. Avoid handing out money to children or to those begging. A more appropriate show of support is to donate pens and pencils to schools or take Polaroid pictures to give-away.

Highlights

Shopping for art. Stroll around Ubud for quirky artefacts, hand-carved furniture and hanging wall pieces.

Mosques, monuments & museums. Discover Java's mystical arts, culture and fabulous museums.

Spa in style. Indulge in a massage, flower bath or body treatment in one of Bali's world class spas.

Beach bum. Explore the dreamy white beaches of Lombok.

Tip for the Trip

"Travel in the low season. If your mind is set on a certain destination, find out when they have their off-season. Some hotels offer significantly lower prices (and you can barter with them) during the off-season. The off-season usually is a time when the weather isn't at its best, but this can mean hotter than normal weather for some locations, or rainy season in others"

Jill

Opposite page. Infinity pool with view of Losari Mountains, Java.

Adventure: Culture + Art
Destination: Java

Regional Information

Indonesia (home to the capital 'Jakarta') provides many contrasts of scenery, people, religions and cultures. The island boasts immense beauty, from peaceful villages and a beautiful, fertile countryside to smoking volcanoes and ancient monuments.

Although Indonesia as a whole is particularly rich in art and culture, which are intertwined with religion and age-old traditions from the time of early migrants with Western thoughts brought by Portuguese traders and Dutch colonists, no-where is this more evident than in Java. Jakarta is a mixed modern city (but can be overcrowded) filled with Dutch architecture, plenty of museums and ancient monuments. South of the mountainous spine in central Java, lies the most popular city in Indonesia, Yogyakarta, the centre for Javanese art and culture, and nearby the astounding Hindu complex and Buddhist monument of Prambanan and Borobudur (which shouldn't be missed). Mount Bromo (which is 2,392 metres) to the east is an active volcano amid stunning scenery which dominates the islands landscape. Active couples can easily climb the mountain (or you can hire a horse to do the hard work!).

Java's Borobudur is one of the continent's most impressive sites, surviving damage from volcanoes, terrorist bombs and hordes of tourists. Built from two million stone blocks in the form of a massive symmetrical stupor, literally wrapped around a small hill, this colossal Buddhist monument remains as enigmatic and beautiful as it must have been 1200 years ago. The paintwork is long gone, but it's thought that the grey stone of Borobudur was at one time washed with a colour to catch the sun. It's so vast you can see the structure from the air if flying over from Bali to Jakarta, so it's wise to allow a couple of days to visit the area to appreciate the monument. The best time to see Borobudur and capture something of the spirit of the temple is at dawn or sunset, but you won't have it to yourself. These are popular times for the bus loads of tour groups to visit Borobudur. The temple is usually at its quietest during Ramadan.

The are many other monuments and museums found throughout the island offering the whole spectrum of Indonesian life, thought and history, beginning from the time of the earliest inhabitation and even before, up to the present. The best known and also the oldest in existence of the museums of art, culture and history is the Central Museum in Jakarta. Museums of natural history are found in Bogor and Bandung.

Jakarta's Central Museum (also known as The Elephant House) is reputedly one of the finest in Southeast Asia. Founded in 1788, it still has the world's most complete collection of Indonesian artefacts. Its Hindu-Javanese collection rivals that of the Leiden Museum in Holland, reputedly the finest in the world. Adjacent to the museum is the National Library with over 700,000 old and recent volumes of books, manuscripts and periodicals covering virtually every subject on Indonesia. It's worth a visit if you are staying in or near Jakarta.

The open-air museum of Old Batavia, now called Jakarta, Taman Fatahillah (Fatahillah Square) has three main establishments standing on the south, east and west of the cobblestone square proper. The first is the Jakarta Museum which exhibits the colonial history of the city and also includes relics from the pre-colonial past. The edifice on the east, formerly the Supreme Court, houses the Fine Arts Gallery and the Ceramics Museum containing, among others, the excellent Chinese and Southeast Asian ceramics collection donated by the late former Vice President, Adam Malik. On the western side of the square is the Wayang Museum, filled with all sorts of puppets used in the indigenous puppet theatre. Demonstrations of the shadow play, lasting two hours, are given every Sunday morning.

Adventure: Culture + Art
Destination: Java

There area approximately one dozen major museums located throughout Yogyakarta. These museums serve to explain and share the culture of the Javanese people with the tourists who come to the area. They also serve to preserve and commemorate the history of the area. Some of the museums to see while in Yogyakarta include:

- Batik Museum – This museum is entirely devoted to the ancient batik art which has spread throughout the world in recent decades.
- Dirgantara Air Museum – World War II was an important time in this area; the museum showcases World War II military aeroplanes, including rare Russian aeroplanes, as well as aeroplanes from other times.
- Kekayon – This is the most famous of the museums which display the wayang puppets which are central to the performing arts culture of the area.
- Kraton (or Keraton) – This historic site includes a museum which describes the area. Perhaps of more interest is that it includes an exhibit of chariots belonging to the sultan who lived here.

Java also boasts a variety of festivals and events held throughout the year. The Ramayana Ballet, Java's most spectacular dance drama, is performed at the outdoor theatre at the Prambanan temple complex on four successive nights, twice a month from May to September. The month long Jakarta Fair in June-July includes carnival attractions and cultural events. Parades are held in every town and village in August to celebrate Independence Day. The island of Madura, just off Java's northeastern coast, stages its famous bull races in August and September. The races culminate with the final race at Pamekasan, usually in September.

Buddhist Vaicak at Borobudur, which celebrates the enlightenment of Buddha is held once a year over the full moon in May or June. Thousands of pilgrims gather to offer prayers and join the procession from the nearby Mendut temple to Borobudur. The 4 day Borobudur Festival is held at the same time and includes dance and music performances and arts and crafts exhibits.

Java offers the visitor a vivid and rewarding experience of an intensely striking land and culture, a tapestry of religions and historical influences, and splendid landscapes that make it the enchanting 'Garden of the East', with a variety of accommodation to suit different levels of luxury (and budgets).

From top. Dalom Jiwo Suite Pool at Amanjiwo. Outdoor bathtub at Amanjiwo. Java Red Restaurant at Losari Coffee Plant

Stylish Places to Stay

A night with nature: Amanjiwo. A tad expensive but worth splashing out. This quiet retreat is surrounded by volcanoes and verdant plantations with a luxurious infinity pool to cool off after a day's sightseeing. The rooms are like mini-temples with every luxury you can imagine – best of all you can also hire bikes to explore the local village.

Javanese jewel: Losari Coffee Plantation. Located a 2 hour drive from Borobudur, (near Magelang) this boutique gem has a private steam train which runs tours through the countryside. The plantation is still producing coffee as well as organic produce which is used in the Losari's restaurant.

Rural retreat: Ijen Resort & Villas. These charming bungalows are located in rural Eastern Java are a breath of fresh air (literally!). They have stunning views of Mount Ijen and across the Bali Strait.

Delicious Places to Eat

Café lounge style: Dixie, Yogyakarta. A cosy place (located in Yogyakarta) with a huge variety of food and live music on the weekends. It's pretty popular with locals and tourists too and the burgers are incredible.

Seafood special: Restoran Boyong Kalegan. An incredible seafood restaurant serving up local, fresh delicacies such as lobster, with an Indonesian twist.

Med-chic: Java Red Restaurant. A more formal spot, combining authentic Indonesian cuisine with hearty Mediterranean dishes, offering splendid forest views.

Opposite page. Honeymoon bath.

Adventure: Spa
Destination: Bali

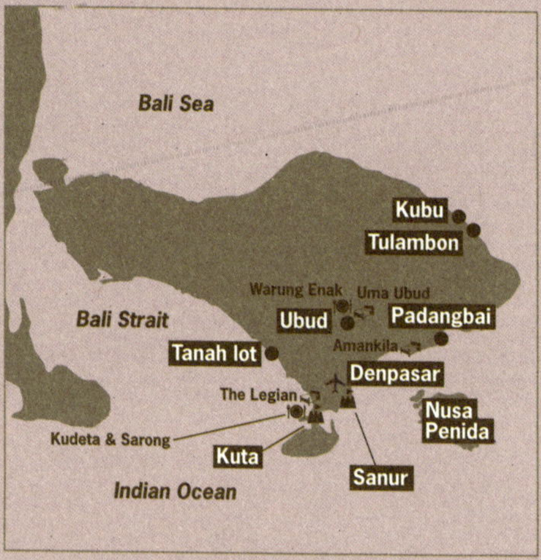

Regional Information

Like many islands, Bali has developed a world of its own. It not only encapsulates what is special about Indonesia but also has a uniqueness of its own. The culture of Bali is unique to the rest of Indonesia. The large majority of the 3,000,000 people of Bali practice a unique religion called Agama Hindu Dharma, unlike the rest of Indonesia where Muslim is dominant. Their religion is deep-rooted in spirituality, which is manifested in their culture as an essential part of daily life. Unlike Hinduism in India, the Balinese have elements of Buddhism, Hinduism, Javanese and indigenous beliefs mixed into their religion. This is still reflected in days to day life and can be seen in the numerous ceremonies, Balinese festivals and magnificent temples and palaces. The Balinese are skilled artisans, particularly in woodcarving which can be seen on the many ornate doorways to houses and hotels.

The Balinese are also noted for their traditional dance, the distinctive music of the gamelan and for their skills in weaving cloth of gold and silver threads, Songket, as well as for embroidering silk and cotton clothing. Stone and woodcarvings, traditional and modern paintings and intricately designed jewellery in gold and silver are readily available in shops and galleries throughout the island. As for recreation, there is no shortage of options. Nature walks, horseback riding, diving, surfing - even bungy jumping and white water rafting - await the adventurous here.

Good diving and snorkelling areas among the reefs are found off the coast of west Bali and those near Padangbai in Eastern Bali, and at Nusa Lembongan on Nusa Penida, the large island off Bali's Southeastern shores (which can be reached as a day trip). There is also a wreck, that of the S.S. Liberty, only 40 metres off the beach at Tulambon, near Kubu.

Adventure: Spa
Destination: Bali

Long walks through the rice fields are a good way for couples to relax and to get a sense of the island's beauty, and meet the locals, who are incredibly friendly. Consider hiring a local driver – ask your hotel for a recommendation – for a half or full day island tour. In Ubud, an ideal home base, you can fill your days with walks, museum visits, musical performances, terrific restaurants and endless shopping. Traditional Balinese music and dance is ever present in Ubud – there is literally something going on every night. Tourist-friendly temple dances include kecak, legong and barong performances and gamelan orchestras, featuring Balinese gongs and percussion instruments, who regularly serenade.

Although Bali is endowed with many activities, it is the world class spas which give Bali its international recognition. Everywhere from the small local salon offering a basic massage, to the extensive treatment programs offered by super luxurious spa resorts. Bali is easily the Spa capital of Asia, if not the world. Body massage has been a part of Balinese culture for many centuries; even most Balinese men go for a Kerok (Bali Massage) on a regular basis. But don't ask for a Kerok unless you are used to it, as it involves painful wooden balls scraping up and down the back. Obviously techniques have been modified, but still provide a deep penetrating massage using elbows and heels of the hands.

There are many different types of massages: Balinese, Indonesian, Thai, Swedish, Shiatsu from Japan and Lomi-Lomi from Hawaii, body wraps, polishes and scrubs (including the Royal Javanese Lulur and the Balinese Boreh), Chinese Reflexology and many Ayurvedic styles of treatment. In the Ubud area some spas offer Craniosacral Therapy and other healing treatments. Double rooms are sometimes offered for couples (especially newlyweds) who wish to share the experience and the Four Hand Massage is very popular too [two therapists, male or female, perform a full body massage in perfect synchronisation].

Although the word 'spa' has developed into a generic term, now used to describe just about anywhere that offers 'treatments', in the 14th century it was generally used to describe places of healing hot springs or resorts located near a source of mineral water. From the very earliest time of the Hindu religion, the site of Tampaksiring, a holy spring which is the source of the Pekerison River, has been sacred to the Balinese. The ritual bathing place, the temples and the beauty of the area bring a continuous stream of islanders as well as visitors. Pools for ritual purification constitute a vital part of the religion and are to be found throughout the island.

Below from top. Dining on the beach, Legian. Beach at Legian. Dining at sunset at Ku de Ta, Courtesy of christopherleggett.com.

Stylish Places to Stay

Isolated & intimate: Amankila. Small, intimate even though its part of the super-luxe Aman resorts group, this spot is pure heaven for honeymooners blowing the budget. The azure infinity pools and the Balinese spa ensure this is top of the list.

Private pad: The Legian. Located in prestigious Seminyak known for its sunsets and perfect beach. All rooms are 'Balinese' styled suites filled with every attention to detail imaginable. Private Butler, day beds, a terrace overlooking the ocean make this hotel addictive, special and very peaceful.

Boutique Balinese retreat: Uma Ubud. Located in arts and crafts centre Ubud, this hip place is a contemporary getaway, with 3 hectares of land at the edge of Tjampuhan Valley. They also offer yoga classes and body treatments from the Shambhala spa.

Delicious Places to Eat

Beachside chic: Ku De Ta. A chic place attracting an attractive crowd of beach lovers. Perfect for sundowners and loved up couples for a romantic meal. After dinner you can even relax on the loungers (and fall asleep), if you want to walk off your meal its only walking distance from The Legian.

Sofas & sexiness: Sarong. New, sensual and romantic is the way this place is marketed. Quite right it is: with lush fabrics lining the walls and organza drapes separating eating areas, this place is a fabulous cosy night in for a romantic couple.

Rattan & eclectic: Warung Enak. At the cultural heart of Ubud, is this casual but chic Balinese restaurant. For those wanting to get to the heart of Indonesian cooking, they also host cookery classes.

Opposite page. Gili Island Beach, Courtesy of Dreamstime.

Adventure: Beach
Destination: Lombok

Regional Information

Lombok island has white virgin beaches, an age-old culture, separated by merely a narrow strait from Bali, it is only now being discovered as a tourist destination of exceptional charm and a renowned 'get away from it all' destination. Here the motto is "you can see Bali in Lombok, but not Lombok in Bali". It is an existing reality, formed by the superimposition of strong Balinese influences in the past, upon a base that is entirely Lombok's own. At around the time Islam first came to these islands in the 16th century, four Hindu Kingdoms coexisted in apparent peace in what is now west Nusa Tenggara. At present, Hinduism is the religion embraced mostly by the Balinese population of Western Lombok. The indigenous people of Lombok, the Sasaks, (which make up the majority) are predominantly Muslim.

Lombok has long been one of Indonesia's poorest islands, (it's much less developed than Bali) but is beginning to reap some rewards from growing tourism since the early 1990's. The majority of villages remain untouched by the influence of visitors and most people are still involved in the day-to-day tasks of farming rice, tobacco, soybeans, corn and peanuts. A few villages scattered through the island are known for high-quality pottery and hand weavings, which can be great buys for visitors. A week exploring the island or relaxing on one of the fine beaches is probably enough to enjoy the best of what the island has to offer.

There are a huge variety of public (and private hotel) beaches both on the mainland Lombok and around the Gili islands.

Batu Bolong beach is located 9 km from downtown Mataram, this beach has a huge rock with a hole in it.

Opposite page. Left. Sunset at the Quinci Villa Hotel. **Right.** Jackfruit Curry.

Adventure: Beach
Destination: Lombok

Kuta beach (not to be confused with the other kuta beach in Bali) also known as Putri Nyale Beach is on the south coast of central Lombok is one of the most scenic and unspoiled beaches in this part of Indonesia. From Kuta to Tanjung Aan 5 km away, is an unbroken stretch of clean white sand on the Indian Ocean. It is safe for bathing and swimming, although further to the west are the surfers and wind surfers beaches. Each year, on the 19th day of the tenth month of the Sasak lunar calendar on February or March when the Nyale fish come to the sea's surface, Kuta Beach is the site of great festivities. Fishermen sail out to sea while young men and women gather along the beach to join in the merrymaking, tease each other and perhaps meet to build a more lasting relationship.

The tropical picture perfect 'Gili islands' (of which there are 3) Gili Trawangan, Gili Meno and Gili Air are renowned scuba-diving destinations. The busiest of the 3 islands is Gili Trawangan, which is also the largest; Gili Air is the second most developed and also the closest to mainland Lombok. Gili Meno is the quietest and secluded with very basic accommodation options. You can reach the islands from Benoa harbour in roughly about 2 hours with a fast boat. All forms of motorized transport are banned from the islands: your only choice is horse-drawn carts, known as cidomo, which are used even to shuttle around diving gear. However, as the islands are only a few km in diameter, it's entirely possible to just walk around.

Over the past decade, each of the three islands has develop a unique personality, catering for different types of travellers. Although the Gili island were previously popular mainly with backpackers, word has spread and the Gili island now attract a diverse range of visitors; serious diving enthusiasts and sun seekers looking for the perfect beach getaway.

The Gilis are small coral islands with sparse vegetation and rainfall, and it can much seem hotter there than the mainland Lombok. Meaning there is sunshine most days of the year. Water is mainly drawn from wells or otherwise shipped from the mainland Lombok, so there is a need for conservation to preserve the limmited resources. Be prepared for salty showers in most of the small hotels. The scuba-diving is really superb, with the opportunity to regularly spot black tip sharks and more than 6,000 species of marine life living just off-shore.

Whilst the beaches might not be as exceptional as they are on mainland Lombok; Gili Trawangan has the nicest physical beaches of the three islands. Gili Meno and Air have their best beaches on the west side of the islands. The south side tends to be windy and rough and the north and east sides have a lot of coral on the beaches, making the sand rough. On Gili Air, the only pleasant beach for swimming is really in front of the Chill-out cafe and Sunrise Hotel on the main strip. Like the rest of Lombok, the islanders are mainly Muslim, so visitors should be respectful of their sensibilities; in particular nude or topless bathing even on the beach is quite offensive to them, even if they won't directly say anything.

Stylish Places to Stay

Opulent luxury: Oberoi. The Oberoi, Lombok resort lies opposite the three Gili Islands – renowned for their colourful coral reefs and dazzling tropical sea life. Fabulous bungalows (some with private plong pools) overlook a lovely sandy beach. The Beach Club offers most popular water sports and scuba diving and there is a gorgeous spa and fully equipped fitness centre on hand, as well as a nearby 18-hole golf course.

Chic retreat: Quinci Villa Hotel. Low-key and small, this hotel has only 20 rooms tastefully decorated with local art – ensuring a couple who doesn't want to be disturbed can relax in peace.

Beach chic: Alang-Alang Boutique Beach Hotel. Located on Senggigi beach with personal service, with a laid back and chilled atmosphere.

Delicious Places to Eat

Local delight: De Quake. Located in Senggigi's Art Market, De Quake features a unique menu of Indonesian and Asian food with fresh fish, seafood, meats and chicken together with fresh produce and local herbs and spices, all at a reasonable price.

Laid-back luxe: Square. Chilled out atmosphere with subdued lighting invite you to relax in comfort, while sipping drinks and listenening to great music, watching the passing parade below on Jl Raya Senggigi.

Surfs up dude: Lombok Lounge. Located next to Matahari Inn. It could be the centre of Kuta nightlife. Best (and possibly cheapest) restaurant in town. They also serve fresh fish cooked to your taste. The owner is incredibly funny and his hospitality wonderful. Many surfers come gravitate here after a day's surf.

Opposite page. Top. Whale Shark.
Bottom. Komodo Dragon. Both courtesy of Dreamstime.

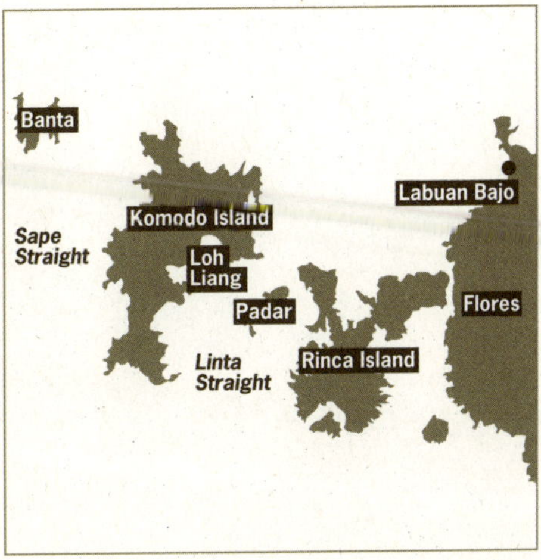

Focus On...
Komodo National Park

The Komodo National Park is a national park located near the Lesser Sunda Islands in the border region between the provinces of east Nusa Tenggara and west Nusa Tenggara. The park includes the three larger islands Komodo, Rinca and Padar, as well as numerous smaller ones, and a total area of 1817 km² (603 km² of it land). The national park was founded in 1980 in order to protect the Komodo dragon, which is the world's largest living specie of lizard, growing to an average of 2-3 metres, and whose ancestors date back over 100 million years. The Komodo has descended and evolved to its present form over 4 million years ago and are first and foremost opportunistic carnivores, and predators second.

In 1991 the national park was named a UNESCO World Heritage Site and is also dedicated to protecting other species, including marine species (such as whale sharks, ocean sunfish, manta rays etc.) The variety of marine life coupled with clear waters makes it an excellent destination for scuba-diving enthusiasts, even for couples who are just interested in snorkeling, the variety and clarity is superb. However the most popular tourist activity is a hike to the Banugulung viewing area, a two-hour roundtrip level walk that originates from Loh Liang. Hikes to other areas of Komodo are also possible, and vary from one to two days: Gunung Ara, Poreng, Loh Sebita, Gunung Sata libo, Soro Masangga. On longer walks overnight accommodation can be arranged at ranger posts at Loh Sebita and Loh Genggo.

While most visitors enter Komodo National Park through the gateway cities of Labuan Bajo, in the west of Flores or Bima in Eastern Sumbawa, the park is also served by a wide range of 'live-aboard' boats with a variety of departure points, including Bali, Lombok, Bima and Labuan Bajo. Alternatively if you are staying nearby (such as the Bajo Eco-lodge or Puri Komodo villas) you can visit Komodo easily on a day trip.

Stylish Essentials

General Information

Tourist Information
www.indonesia-tourism.com

Airlines

British Airways
www.ba.com
T. 0844 493 0 787
(UK reservations & enquiries)

Qantas
www.qantas.com.au
T. 0845 7747 767
(UK reservations number)

Singapore Airlines
www.singaporeair.com
T. 0844 800 2380 (UK reservations)
T. +44 (0) 208 961 6993
(Outside UK Reservations)

Merpati
www.merpati.co.id
T. +62 (0) 21 65 48 888
(Reservations)

Silk Air
www.silkair.com
T. +65 (0) 6223 8888
(Singapore Reservations)

Ferries

Penguin ferries
Singapore to Batam
www.penguin.com
E. reservation@penguin.com.sg

Pelni ferries
www.pelni.co.id
T. +62 (0) 21 79 18 06 06
(Call centre)

ASDP Fast Ferries
Connecting Nusa Tenggara with Bali and Surabaya in Java as well as from Surabaya to Kalimantan.
www.ferry-asdp.co.id/english.

Bounty Cruises
Benoa Harbour
T. +62 (0) 361 72 66 66
E. info@baliboutycruises.com
www.balibountycruises.com
Open: 7.30–21.00

Bali

Scuba Diving

BIDP
Jl. Danau Poso 26
Sanur 80228
Bali
www.bidp-balidiving.com
T. +62 (0) 36 12 70 759

Spa Guide
www.balispaguide.com

Surf Lessons
Pro Surf School Bali
Jl. Pantai Kuta, Kuta,
Bali 80032
www.prosurfschool.com
T. +62 (0) 361 744 1466

Uma Ubud
Jalan Raya Sanggingan, Banjar Lungsiakan,
Kedewatan
Ubud, Bali
www.theumaubud.com
T. +62 (0) 361 972 448

The Legian
Jalan Laksmana,
Seminyak Beach
Bali
www.ghmhotels.com
T. +62 (0) 361 730 622

Amankila
Manggis,
Karangesam, Bali,
www.amanresorts.com
T. +62 (0) 363 41333

Ku De Ta
Jalan Laksmana No.9
Seminyak, Bali
www.kudeta.net
T. +62 (0) 361 73 6767

Sarong
Jl. Petitenget, No.19X
Kerobokan, Kuta
www.sarongbali.com
T. +62 (0) 361 737 809

Warung Enak
Ubud, Bali
T. +62 (0) 361 97 29 11
www.warungenakbali.com

Java

Borobudur Temple
Located 25 miles Northwest of Yogyakarta
Transport: Inclusive tour from Yogya, or local bus from Yogya's Umbulharjo bus station
www.borobudurpark.com
T. + 62 (0) 293 788266 (info)
Open: 06.00–17.00

Bromo-Tengger-Semerus National Park
Mt Bromo
Jl..Intan No 6, Malang, East Java
T. + 62 (0) 341 41828 (Park office)

National Museum (Gedung Gajah – Elephant House)
Jl. Merdeka Barat 12, Jakarta
T. + 62 (0) 21 386 8172 (info)
Open: Tue-Thu, Sun 8.30–14.30, Fri 08.30–11.30, Sat 08.30–01.30
Tours: Tue, Wed, Thu mornings, in a number of languages

Taman Fatahillah (Fatahillah Square)
Batavia's Town Square
Jalan Pintu Besar Utara
Kota
Jakarta, 11110
T. +62 (0) 21 315 4094

Ramayana Ballet
Visit www.yogyes.com for more information

Jakarta Fair
Held at Jakarta International Expo
www.jakartafair.biz (English version also available)

Independence Day
Held on August 17th every year

Bull Races
Held twice a month during September through to October and generally start at 9am in the towns of Bangkalan, Sampang and Pameksan.

Buddhist Vaicak at Borobudur
www.borobudurcorners.com

Amanjiwo
Borobudur, Magelang,
Central Java
www.amanresorts.com
T. +62 (0) 293 788 333

Losari Coffee Plantation
Desa Losari - Grabag PO Box 108
Magelang 56100
Central Java
www.losaricoffeeplantation.com
T. +62 (0) 298 596333

Restoran Boyong Kalegan
J.L. Pakem Turi Sleman, Yogyakarta
T. +62 (0) 274 897055
E. admin@boyongkalegan.com

Java Red Restaurant
(see Losari Coffe plantation for details)

Ijen Resort & Villas
Randu Agung, Banyuwangi
East Java
www.ijendiscovery.com
T. +62 (0) 333 429000

Dixie Yogakarta
Jl. Gejayan No. 40b Seletan Selokan
Mataram
T. +62 (0) 274 560745

Lombok

Blue Marlin Dive Centre
The Gili Islands
www.bluemarlindive.com
T. + 62 (0) 370 632424

Gili Islands Information
T. +62 (0) 361 753241
www.gili-paradise.com

Blue Water Safaris in Lombok
Gili island Adventures
T. + 62 (0) 8133 841 8988
info@bwsbali.com
www.bwsbali.com

Oberoi
Medana Beach, Tanjung, Mataram
Lombok
83001
www.oberoihotels.com
T. +62 (0) 370 638 444

Quinci Villa Hotel
Jalan Raya Mangsit,
Senggigi, Lombok
www.quincivillas.com
T. +62 (0) 370 693 800

Alang-Alang Boutique Beach Hotel
Jl. Raya Mangsit Senggigi
Senggigi - Mataram 83355
Lombok
www.alang-alang-villas.com
T. +62 (0) 370 693 518

De Quake
Art Market,
Senggigi, Lombok
www.dequake.com
T. +62 (0) 370 693 694

Square
Square Restaurant & Lounge, Blok B
No. 10, Jl. Raya Senggigi Km. 08,
Senggigi, west Lombok
www.squarelombok.com
T. +62 (0) 370 6645999

Lombok Lounge
Located next to Matahari Inn.

Sumbawa

General Information
www.sumbawa.org

Komodo National Park

General Information
Komodo Office
Gg. Mesjid, Kampung Cempa,
Labuan Bajo
Manggarai Barat, Nusa Tenggara
Timur
www.komodonationalpark.org
T. + 62 (0) 385 41448
T. + 62 (0) 385 41225
info@putrinagakomodo.com

Komodo Park Live aboard Cruise
www.seasafaricruises.com
info@seasafaricruises.com

Puri Komodo Bungalows
Batu Gosok - west Flores
www.purikomodoresort.com

Bajo Eco Lodge
Jl. Pantai Pede Km.
Gorontalo-Labuan, Flores
www.ecolodgeindonesia.com
T. +62 (0) 385 41391

Night scene in Tokyo.

uman
さくらや
西口駅前店
さくらや
駅前留学
NOVA
5F

JAPAN

Tokyo | Kyoto | Hakone | Hokkaido |

Why is this place so special?

Japan is pretty distinctive. The traditional customs and codes of behaviour aren't like anywhere else, the creativity displayed by fashion conscious youths and by quirky hotels are like something off this planet. And where in the world can you go and sing karaoke until the early hours, eat raw fish that might poison you and wear wooden sandals with socks? Japan is certainly not for those who take life too seriously, and it's perfect for couples wanting something quirky, adventurous and culturally rich.

Whilst Japan might not be considered a normal honeymoon destination, it is nevertheless a fantastic choice for couples wanting a trip that involves observing local culture, exploring stunning mountains, gardens, palaces, volcanoes and bathing in hot spas. The country also offers superb cuisine, fascinating architecture and many natural and historical sites.

The bustling capital, Tokyo, is alive with energy. It has countless monuments and a plethora of unusual buildings and hotels created by innovative architects. Some of these creations are minimalist, others are highly detailed, but they all have an unmistakably Japanese style. Tokyo also offers superb shopping in chic arcades, and many galleries and museums where you will be able to admire distinctive Japanese art. You can choose between sake (rice wine), shochu (shoju) or traditional green tea to accompany your meal in one of the city's many restaurants. Perfectly symmetrical Mount Fuji is the highest mountain in Japan (which can be seen and visited in a day from Tokyo or Hakone) and attracts visitors from far and wide. The summit offers spectacularly romantic vistas, particularly as dawn breaks.

Top. Wedding in Kyoto. **Bottom.** Japanese Garden in Kyoto.

Kyoto is considered the imperial heart of Japan, and remains the cultural centre of the country, home to hundreds of festivals every year, countless temples and precisely designed gardens scattered across the city. Kyoto is the centre of the mysterious and artisanal 'Geisha' community with 'Gion Corner' and several shrines to witness ceremonies from tea making to weddings. Hakone is famous for hot springs, so couples wanting pampering and to experience the ancient Japanese ritual of bathing, should find this appealing. It is also popular for local Japanese, wanting a break from the city as the national park is right on the doorstep, providing a healthy dose of fresh air and activities for stressed out city dwellers.

Japan is so rich and endowed with adventures, it would make sense to spend at least a couple of weeks travelling and exploring, and perhaps a few night relaxing in the countryside. The variety of accommodation is immense from 'Love hotels' to traditional 'Ryokans' so couples will find something for their taste and budget.

Fast Facts

Capital: Tokyo.

Location: An island chain with no other land boundaries, located in Eastern Asia, situated between the North Pacific Ocean and the Sea of Japan and East of the Korean Peninsula.

Population: 127,288,419.

Religion: Shinto and Buddhist 84%, other 16% (including Christian 0.7%).

Languages: Japanese.

Getting there and exploring around

While most people fly via Tokyo, there are other ways of getting to and from Japan. There are several airports in Japan (Osaka, Fukuoka etc) some of which make better entry points than Tokyo's Narita international airport. It is also possible to arrive in Japan by sea from a number of nearby countries, in particular South Korea. Travelling around by ferry in Japan, while slow, can be pleasant and relaxing. The main routes are from Osaka/Kobe (on Honshu) to Beppu/Oita (on Kyushu), Niigata on the Japan Sea coast to Otaru/Sapporo (Hokkaido), Sendai to Tomokomai in southern Hokkaido and the ferry route connecting Japan with Korea. The cheapest accommodation is in often cramped, communal, large tatami-mat rooms, so if you are looking for something more intimate then book a private cabin (some of them even have baths!).

Flying is a more efficient way to travel from the main islands to the small islands, Check whether you qualify for discounts - there are some weird and wonderful ones (for example JAL offers discounts for three or more women travelling together, or for a husband and wife if their combined age totals 88 or more) and Japan Air Passes do exist to make air travel cheaper. JAL (Oneworld) and ANA (Star Alliance) are each offering air passes for exclusive use by foreign visitors to Japan, which enable holders to fly anywhere within Japan for around 12,000 Yen per flight. This is an excellent price on many domestic routes, especially on longer flights, such as from Tokyo to Kyushu, Okinawa or Hokkaido. Like the Japan Rail Pass, air passes have to be purchased outside of Japan, before you leave.

By far the best way to travel around Japan is by train. The trains are fast, frequent, clean and comfortable with services ranging from small local lines to the shinkansen super-expresses, or 'bullet trains'. The Japan Rail Pass provides excellent value for money; allowing unlimited rail & bus travel throughout Japan, but must be purchased before arrival and collected from one of the 'exchange offices'. You can purchase a 'Green Car' ticket (which is first class) for 7, 14 or 21 days from £135. Driving in Japan is also feasible and pleasant outside the major cities, most signs are in English and drivers tend to be considerate.

Best time of year to visit

Japan has quite a different climate to its Asian neighbours, warmer temperatures the more south you go, and cooler temperatures to the north. Spring (March to May), with its clear skies and cherry blossoms, is probably the most celebrated Japanese season. The 'Hanamai' which is a cherry blossom viewing party takes place during April to March for only 2 weeks and it's busy with locals as well as tourists in the countryside.

Summer (June to August) is pretty hot and humid (average temperature is about 28°C (83°F) but the festivals (such as Hanabi Taikai – one of the major fireworks displays in Tokyo on the last Saturday of July and Gion Matsuri festival in Kyoto) can make it a compelling time to visit, and its considered to be 'low-season' so prices are generally cheaper.

Autumn (September to November) is a good time to travel as the temperatures are pleasant, and the autumn colours in the countryside are fantastic. Mid-winter (December to February) can be very cold, especially high up in the mountains.

? Must know before you go

Basic etiquette. In comparison to the relatively 'straightforward' basic rules of Western etiquette, Japanese social customs may appear complex. It would be difficult to cover all aspects of Japanese etiquette, but you should be aware of some very basic rules to help you retain a respectful standing during your stay; age, seniority, honour and understanding the subtext of what people are saying are some of the most important aspects of Japanese culture.

Bowing & introductions. The standard form of greeting in Japan is to bow from the waist – generally, the lower you bow, the more respect is being demonstrated. In most formal and social situations, you should address Japanese people by their title and their surname. Personal space is a great consideration, so try and keep three or four foot away from your acquaintance. Japanese people are not direct talkers as it is considered too crass. You may find that your conversations are punctuated with drawn out silences whilst they are considering all that is being said, and any hidden meanings.

Saving face. Honour and saving or giving face is an important aspect of Japanese culture. The Japanese are notoriously humble and modest people, and respect this kind of humility in others. Never, ever publicly disgrace or humiliate someone in Japan.

Japanese visits. When entering a Japanese house (or Ryokan), you should remove your shoes at the entrance. You may be given some slippers to wear, but just wearing your socks is also acceptable. During a meal, you may share your dishes with other dinner party members, although you should be aware that it is considered bad etiquette to share food with the 'used' end of your chopsticks. Burping at the table is considered vulgar, but slurping your food is not.

Highlights

Bright lights big city Tokyo. Explore the malls, incredible restaurants, stylish bars and stay in a state-of the art hotel.

Culture in Kyoto. Stay in a traditional Ryokan and explore some of the hidden corners of the mysterious 'Geisha' world.

Spas in Hakone. Bathe in the ancient hot springs and relax with a spa treatment.

Outdoors of Hokkaido. Take a breath of fresh air and enjoy the great outdoors in the Daisetsuzan national park.

Tip for the Trip

"Figure out the local tipping customs before you travel. For example in Japan it isn't commonplace to tip and may embarrass (and offend) your host if you offer them your change."

Jill

Opposite page. Japan water cleansing outside Meiji jingu shrine, Tokyo.

Adventure: City
Destination: Tokyo

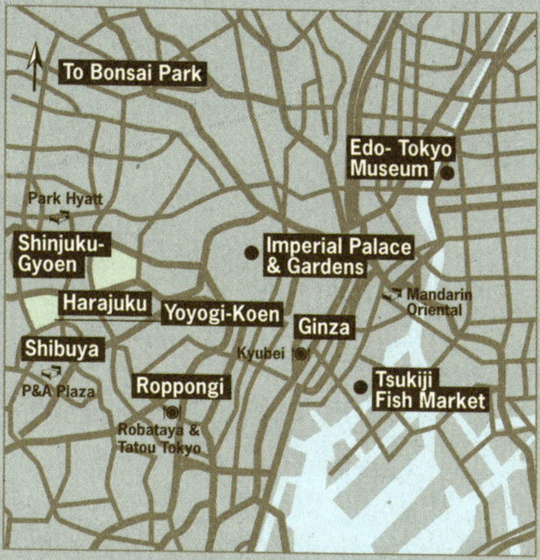

Regional Information

Tokyo is often the first destination for many international travellers to Japan, and one that leaves a lasting impression. The first thing visitors notice is the blend of old and new, cutting edge technology and centuries old shrines. Rowdy, traditional festivals and the spirit of the old Edo period still survive in the neon-bathed entertainment districts: modern-day 'floating worlds' of karaoke and cinemas, shot bars and bathhouses. Traditional kabuki theater thrives alongside opera, ballet and symphonic performances, and Tokyoites are passionate about sumo, baseball and now, thanks partly to the 2002 World Cup, football. With the latest figures estimating an incredible 60,000 eateries in Tokyo and home to the world's largest fish market, food is an obsession even closer to Japanese hearts. A week is ample time to explore Tokyo and its surrounds, but 4 or 5 days might be enough to visit the highlights before hopping to the countryside for some rest & relaxation.

Shopping in Tokyo is a feast; from the designer brands located in Omotesando to street fashion in Harajuku the sheer diversity is remarkable. There are department stores and malls aplenty but, happily, the Japanese and local governments have long been fiercely protective of local shopkeepers, meaning plenty of individuality and variety. The best way to explore Tokyo's shopping is by foot and by each region, that way you can observe as much the culture as well as gawp in shop windows. Omotesando is a major up-market shopping avenue in Harajuku, where most internally known fashion brands have stores, from Dolce & Gabbana to Ralph Lauren and of the incredible state-of-the-art 'Prada' store made with pure steel and glass. This is the world of real brand names so no cheap copies here. Not only is the street full of cafés and international brand clothing boutiques, but now features the very up market shopping centre (Omotesando Hills). The Ginza district is home to Tokyo's oldest and most prestigious department stores; the most well-known is probably Wako Department Store. Wako is considered by some to be the most exclusive department store in

Japan, located at the heart of the district and is famous for its watches, jewellery, porcelain, and handbags, as well as foreign luxury goods. There is also an art gallery, called Wako Hall, on the sixth floor. The Ginza district is home to Mitsokoshu, Matsuzakaya Department Store, Seibu Department store and Sony & Apple megastores, so it's a great location for technology shopping. Shinjuku is also another mecca for department stores, where famous Isetan and Takashimaya Times Square (a giant shopping complex) can be found.

Harajuku famous for its Harajuku Girls (girls dressed up in Gothic chic costumes and little bo-peep), is a popular shopping spot for young people to hang-out at weekends. You can easily find inexpensive clothes, accessories and second hand items here. La Forêt is not only the largest store in Harajuku but also one of the most fashionable, appealing mostly to teenagers and 20-something fashionistas. Young and upcoming Japanese designers are here as well as established names, in boutiques spread on several floors, so 'fashion followers' can easily pick up a few bargains. Oriental Bazaar is also another Tokyo institution stocking everything from kamikaze T-shirts to chopsticks and gaijin-sized kimonos plus a large range of English language books on Japanese design and culture. This is definitely the easiest way to get your souvenir shopping done. Flea markets are still popular here with 'Togo Shrine flea market' having the largest contingent of dealers, where you can find a plethora of antiques. It has numerous stalls in the shrine's garden and you can take a leisurely stroll around and absorb the various sights and sounds. Yoyogi Park flea market is also worth a look and its set in a wonderful park (one of the largest in Tokyo).

Adventure: City
Destination: Tokyo

Most visitors to Harajuku often come here to see Yoyogi Park and Meiji Jingu shrine which are both relaxing spots for picnics and walks. The Meiji Jingu Shrine is one of the most popular shrines in Tokyo (with a forest of 120,000 trees and 175 acres) and is a must see for anyone visiting Tokyo. Not only is this shrine easy to access via train to Harajuku Station, it is also right next to Harajuku, which makes it easy to string together a visit to central Shibuya, Harajuku and Meiji Jingu Shrine all in one day or an afternoon if you really rush it.

The Imperial Palace in Kokyo (the current residence of Japan's imperial family) is located on the former site of Edo Castle, a wonderful large park area surrounded by moats and massive stone walls. Although the palace buildings and inner gardens are not open to the public, visitors can enter on January 2 (New Year's Greeting) and December 23 (Emperor's Birthday), where members of the Imperial Family, make several public appearances on a balcony. The rest of the year tourists can visit the external grounds easily by walking 10 minutes from Toyko station. Guided tours of the palace are offered in Japanese, with an English pamphlet and audio guide provided, tours must be reserved in advance with the Imperial Household Agency.

As night falls there isn't a shortage of things to do. There are plenty of stylish bars, live music venues, clubs and of course the famous karaoke. Roppongi hills is a safe bet for stylish hangouts and the infamous Robataya restaurant. Karaoke singing is usually done in small private rooms, with plush seating and excellent sound systems. Venues are scattered across the city, so you will never be far from a karaoke bar. If you want to splash a bit more cash, the Keio Plaza hotel in Shinjuku hires out top floor rooms from just over 5,000 Yen an hour. They can seat up to 10 and you can enjoy spectacular views of the city at night. The more adventurous karaoke fans head for Lovenet, where singing takes place within a Jacuzzi. Places to stay in Tokyo are often experiences in themselves. Japanese 'love hotels' are an institution; sometimes known as 'fashion' or 'couples hotels' they offer rooms (which are often themed) by the hour or longer, it's not a new concept, yet like all things Japanese the execution isn't sleazy, but fun and quite upscale. In a country (or city, in the case of places like Tokyo) where space is at a premium and not everyone has moved out of their parents, love hotels offer a chance for couples to be together. Ranging from functional to funky, the hotels are identified by excessive neon and often unintentionally funny names. Many travellers are now using love hotels as cheap alternatives to other lodging; so you may well find a bunch of backpackers staying there. For honeymooners staying in a 'love hotel' it can be fun if you keep an open mind, although it's not for prudish couples. Sex toys and condoms are available in vending machines, mirrors line the ceilings, bathtubs are built for two and, some cater to specific sexual indulgence. The rooms are chosen and paid for with the anonymity of the guest in mind. The experience of staying here is like no other.

Below from left. Tranquility Suite at the Spa of the Hotel Mandarin Oriental, Tokyo. Robataya.

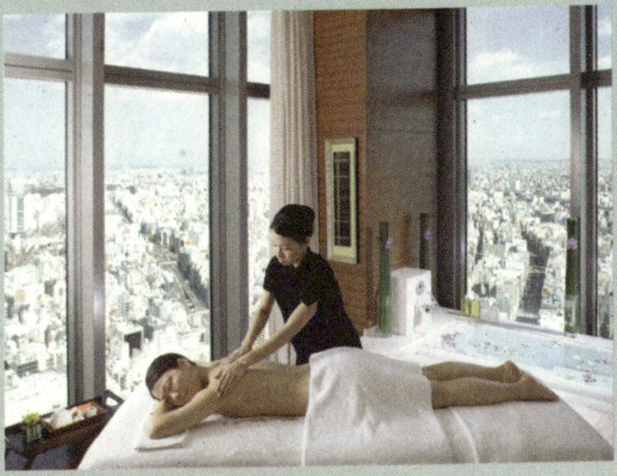

Stylish Places to Stay

Lost in the sky: Park Hyatt. Located in west-Shinjuku, the giant granite tower, has a superb bar on the 52nd floor overlooking the city's skyline. It's no wonder the movie makers for 'Lost in Translation' choose to film here. All rooms have original artwork and bathrooms are to die for, kitted out with TV's, sunken tubs and toilets you need to read manual to work them out.

Spa escape: Mandarin Oriental. Another giant tower with fabulous views of the city. What makes this places stand out are the warm Asian hospitality, and decorative Japanese textiles furnished throughout. The 'sense tea corner' offering couples a bit more intimacy and privacy serving a luscious afternoon tea, while the spa offers a range of wonderful treatments.

Loved-up love hotel: P&A Plaza. Located in Shibuya, if you want to pretend you're Hugh Hefner in the Playboy Grotto then room 902 is the place to do it. There's also a party room (room 801) that holds up to 20 people for couples who want more space. Room 805 has exercise machines and a tanning bed. There's also a room with a swimming pool. You can choose themed rooms from neo-Japanesque to Moroccan style.

Delicious Places to Eat

Sushi in the city: Kyubei. Pretty and traditional Japanese style eatery, located in busy business district Ginza, serving the best sushi & shashimi in Toyko. All the menus are in Japanese but the chefs will explain the choices to you.

Fun & friendly: Robataya. A unique restaurant with plenty of atmosphere to keep you entertained for an entire evening. Although expensive it's worth the trip especially when staff greet you by yelling IRASSHAIMASE (welcome), you feel like a celebrity being announced. Food is laid out like a traditional buffet with the chefs kneeling in the centre, just point to the food you want, they cook it, and pass it to you on a paddle. Try the kobe beef and wash down with different strengths of sake and shoju.

Private party: Tatou Tokyo. Private booths line the sides of Tatou's theatrical main floor, allowing diners a view of the live music on stage. If you're after some privacy, ask for the upper circle bar, where the staff will discretely draw a red velvet curtain to close off your booth. Away from prying eyes you'll be able to enjoy a quiet cocktail and a view down to the dining room.

Oppostie page. Geisha Girls in Kyoto.

Adventure: Culture + Art
Destination: Kyoto

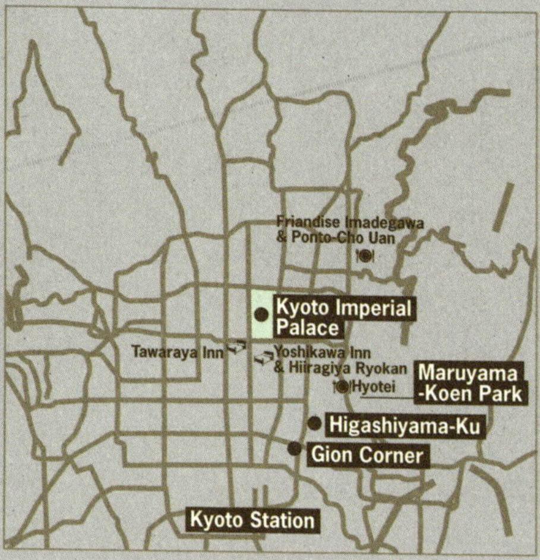

Regional Information

Kyoto is a stunning city and is believed to be the imperial heart of Japan. Kyoto was Japan's capital and the emperor's residence between 794A.D and 1868. It is now the country's seventh largest city with a population of 1.4 million people and is one of the most visited cities in Japan. Over the centuries, many wars and fires destroyed Kyoto, but due to its historic value, the city was not chosen as a target of air raids during World War II. Countless temples, shrines and other historically priceless structures still survive in the city today, making it a prefect destination for honeymooners looking for a rich cultural experience. A week should be long enough to explore Kyoto's sights and surrounds.

Travellers who land here have often been inspired after seeing movie epic Arthur Goldens' 'Memoirs of a Geisha', where you can still visit several Kyoto locations featured in the film, such as Yoshimine-dera Temple, Kiyomizu-dera Temple, Fushimi Inari Shrine, Heian Shrine, the bamboo forest in Arashiyama (on the outskirts of Kyoto) and the geisha district of Gion. The Gion Corner, is one of the most famous 'Geisha'districts, where you are likely to catch a glimpse of one or even more likely a trainee Geisha, often known as a 'maiko'.

The Gion Corner theatre hosts evening entertainment where visitors can watch a typical tea ceremony, flower arranging and puppeteer theatre. It typically lasts about 2 hours and visitors gain a short insight into the arts and rituals of this hidden world. Theatre performances usually take place in the evening and together with an evening meal in the 'Gion' district make a great night out. Other cultural experiences, such as home visits, cookery, and Japanese language and origami classes can be arranged by several companies in Kyoto, most noted is Wak Japan where learning takes place in a typical Japanese house. It's ideal for couples wanting to gain a more in-depth insight into Japanese culture and traditions.

There are literally thousands of Buddhist temples and hundreds of Shinto shrines in Kyoto to explore. Like temples, shrines are places of worship and the dwellings of 'Kami', or Gods. Where the shrine differs from the temple is that Shinto has upwards of 8 million gods to be worshipped. People pray at shrines for protection from evil, for the safety and prosperity of their families, and for the success of their business, among other things. Buddhism was first introduced from Korea in the late 6th century was instituted as the state religion by Prince Shotoku (574-622). In 794, Emperor Kammu moved the capital from Nara to Nagaoka (a suburb of Kyoto), and a decade later shifted it to present-day Kyoto. In accordance with a policy barring temples from the central capital, the temples were built on or at the base of surrounding mountains.

The largest and most famous temple in Kyoto is Kiyomizu-dera temple (meaning Pure Water Temple) located on the west side of Kyoto, it is one of the most celebrated temples of Japan. The temple offers visitors beautiful views over the city from its famous wooden terrace and below the terrace; you can taste the pure spring water, which gives the temple its name.

Further West stands the Yoshimine-dera temple which was founded in 1029 by the priest Gensan. It has an ancient pine tree known as Yuryu-matsu standing in the grounds which was planted some 400 years ago. In 1932 it was registered as a Natural Monument, although once much larger the tree has been pruned several times due to infestation by insects. While it is just over 2 metres high today supported branches extend 20 metres each in opposite directions. The tree is said to resemble a dragon. The herbal baths at Yoshimine-dera Temple are said to be beneficial for neuralgia sufferers, as is praying to Kannon at the main hall; hence Yoshimine-dera's nickname, "Neuralgia Temple."

Adventure: Culture + Art
Destination: Kyoto

The most important shrines in Kyoto include Kamigamo-jinja and Shimogamo-jinja, which enshrine water gods, and Yasaka-jinja, at which the god who protects people from epidemics is worshipped. The Yasaka Shrine is also known as Gion Shrine and is famous for the Gion Matsuri, one of Japan's largest festivals. It is located at the eastern end of Shijo-dori and is one of the city's most popular shrines. The many lanterns that decorate the shrine's stage are lit after dark and bear the names of their sponsors, mostly Kyoto businesses.

Inari shrine is home to the god of commerce, and at Kitano-Tenmangu the god of learning is enshrined. Last but not least is Heian Shrine, which enshrines Emperors Kammu and Komei, the founding emperor of Kyoto and the last emperor to reign from Kyoto, respectively. Shrines consist of a torii, (the large entrance gates which is usually orange), a haiden, or oratory, and a honden, the main hall where gods are enshrined. The honden of Ujigamo shrine is the oldest of its kind in Japan, and is pretty spectacular. Fushimi-inari shrine has more than 1,000 toriis, and was filmed during the famous scene in 'Memoirs of a Geisha', where the young Sayuri places a wish to become a geisha. There are 4km of red Shinto gates, which created striking images in the film's closing and opening scenes. This Shrine is famous for its huge gardens graced with beautiful flowers that can be enjoyed throughout the year.

Other 'green' escapes from the bustle of the city are plentiful in Kyoto. Located next to the Yasaka Shrine in is the Maruyama Koen (a public park), with lots of atmosphere at the weekends (you can watch locals playing baseball) and take a picnic. It is also Kyoto's most popular spot for enjoying cherry blossoms in the Spring. Maruyama Koen becomes Kyoto's most popular and most crowded spot for cherry blossom viewing parties (hanami). The centrepiece of the park is a tall shidarezakura (weeping cherry tree), which gets lit up in the night, making it pretty atmospheric and romantic. Equally the Kyoto Imperial palace park is delightful.

A short drive away from Kyoto is the rural forest area of Arashiyama, where there are numerous walks through the stunning Sagano bamboo groves and a riverbed which runs from Nakanoshima district to Matsuobashi. The park has spectacular views of Mount Arashiyama from the famous and romantic "Moon Crossing Bridge" (Togetsukyo). The mountain and park is also home to hundreds of monkeys, which you can approach as they have become fairly accustomed to humans.

Below left. Yoshlkawa Inn. **Right.** Haute cuisine fish in Kyoto.

Stylish Places to Stay

Imperial charm: Tawaraya. A distinguished, venerable old inn, (with an impressive list of celebrity guests) which has been owned and operated by the same family since it opened in the first decade of the 1700s (the present owner, Mrs. Toshi Okazaki Sato, is the 11th generation of innkeepers). Each room has glass sliding doors opening onto a mossy garden of bamboo, stone lanterns, and manicured bushes, with cushions on a wooden veranda where you can sit and soak in the peacefulness.

Quaint & calm: Yoshikawa Inn. For an authentic Japanese experience, this wonderful Ryokan is oozing with charm, character and impeccable service. Very comfortable Tatami rooms with en-suite bathrooms and a fabulous 'Tempura' restaurant. The finely manicured Japanese gardens are delightful as is the impeccable service. Prices include all meals and all socks and slippers!

Fine & fun: Hiiragiya Ryokan. Founded in 1818 is one of Kyoto oldest and finest luxury Ryokans serving Kyoto-style Kaiseki cuisine, which is also included in the room rate. It has 'family baths' and if you want some privacy where you can reserve a time for two.

Delicious Places to Eat

Patisserie picnic: Friandise Imadegawa. What rice is to the Japanese, proper hard bread is to most Europeans. If you are planning on a picnic in the park try this little bakery called Friandise (that's French for "sweets") on Imadegawa Dori. This bread shop, a branch of the main store in Kitaoji, is run by the exceedingly charming Ms. Noriko Hori and staff who offer friendly service and a variety of bread that would make any true connoisseur's heart beat faster.

Romantic & chic: Ponto-Cho Uan. An elegant Kaiseki (Japnese haute cuisine) restaurant, which has a great platform for riverside dining in the summer.

Tea time: Hyotei. Located West of Shirakawa Dori, this 380 year old entrance way of this restaurant, which was once a Japanese tea shop, and the traditional thatched roof of the inner-building provide the background in which guests can enjoy a quiet, private meal overlooking a garden and pond. The Kaiseki served here is the authentic cuisine of the Japanese tea ceremony.

Opposite page. Clockwise from top left. Lake Ashi, Courtesy of Dreamstime. Ancient Cedar Avenue. Mount Fuji.

Adventure: Spa
Destination: Hakone

Regional Information

Hakone is part of the Fuji-Hakone-Izu National Park, less than 100 kilometers from Tokyo, (about 1 hour by train) and although it can be visited in a day, a week staying here is an ideal getaway for loved up couples. Famous for hot springs, (known as Onsens) outdoor activities, natural beauty and the view of nearby Mount Fuji, Hakone is one of the most popular destinations among Japanese and international travellers looking for a break from bustling Tokyo.

Hakone has been one of Japan's leading hot spring resorts for centuries. Nowadays, more than a dozen springs provide hot spring water to the many bath houses and Ryokans in the Hakone region. Onsens (hot springs) are an age-old Japanese tradition drawing couples, families or company groups who want to get away from the hectic life of the city to relax. Japanese often talk of the virtues of 'naked communion' for breaking down barriers and getting to know people in the relaxed atmosphere. People often travel to Onsens with work colleagues, to help break down some of the hierarchical stiffness inherent in Japanese work life. Traditionally, Onsens were located outdoors, although a large number of inns have now built indoor bathing facilities as well. Onsen by definition use naturally hot water from geothermally-heated springs, however, they should be differentiated from a 'Sento', which are indoor public bath houses in the city where the baths are filled with heated tap water. Onsen water is believed to have healing powers derived from its mineral content. A particular Onsen may feature several different baths, each with water with a different mineral composition. The outdoor bath tubs are most often made from Japanese cypress, marble or granite, while indoor tubs may be made with tile, acrylic or stainless steel. Many bathers come for an hour or so to soak in the waters, and some Onsens offer massage treatments too.

Opposite page. Top. Hotel Hakone.
Bottom. Sushi, Courtesy of Dreamstime.

Adventure: Spa
Destination: Hakone

There are various elements of etiquette that should be observed when using an Onsen. Guests are expected to thoroughly wash themselves before entering the hot water, as Onsens are for 'cleansing', they are for relaxing. Onsen guests generally bring a small towel with them to use as a washcloth. The towel can also provide a modicum of modesty when walking between the washing area and the baths. Some Onsens allow you to wear the towel into the baths, while others have posted signs prohibiting this, saying that it makes it harder to clean the bath. In this latter case, people normally set their towels off to the side of the water when enjoying the baths. However, some people place their folded towels on top of their heads.

Yumoto, at the entrance to the Hakone area near Odawara, is Hakone's most famous hot spring area with a particularly long history, high quality water and numerous baths and inns. Tenzan is a collection of nice hot spring pools, mostly outdoors at the foot of a wooded slope and the bath house is a beautiful traditional Japanese style building. A short walk from Miyanoshita station is Rakuyujurin Shizenkan, with outdoor baths on wooden terraces. But many more hot spring baths can be found in the valleys and mountains of Hakone and at the shores of Lake Ashi.

Yunessun is an aquatic theme situated in a natural setting with a multitude of traditional Onsens (outdoor pools), there are even some filled with unusual liquids such as coffee (to assist fatigued skin), red wine (Cleopatra allegedly bathed in it), green tea (to enhance the immune system) and Japanese sake rice wine (they say it increases the skin's beauty). Obviously there is a sign in Japanese and English, "Do not drink". For more privacy you can enter the Mori No Yu zone where the baths are sectioned into private areas and you are supposed to enjoy the experience 'Japanese style' – without your swimsuit.

Lake Ashi (Japanese: Ashinoko) was formed in the caldera of Mount Hakone after the volcano's last eruption 3000 years ago. Today, the lake with Mount Fuji in the background is the symbol of Hakone. The best views of the lake in combination with Mount Fuji can be enjoyed from Moto-Hakone, from the Hakone Detached Palace Garden and from the sightseeing boats cruising the lake. The more adventurous can hike up Mount Fuji, but with more than 6 different ascents and descents, and taking 6 hours to reach the summit, unless you having hiking experience, take a guide with you. Note however, that clouds and poor visibility often block the view of Mount Fuji, and you have to consider yourself lucky if you get a clear view of the mountain. Visibility tends to be better during the colder seasons of the year than in summer, and in the early morning and late evening hours. Two companies, Hakone Sightseeing Boats and Izuhakone Sightseeing Boats, operate boats between Moto-Hakone and Hakone-machi at the lake's southern shores and Togendai and Kojiri at the northern shores. A boat cruise from one end of the lake to the other takes roughly 30 minutes and costs 970 Yen and can be a wonderful romantic experience. The Hakone Free Pass is valid on the pirate ship shaped Hakone Sightseeing Boats but not on boats operated by Izuhakone.

Stylish Places to Stay

Relais & chateaux: Gora Kadan. A luxury ryokan with open air baths and steam rooms carved out of stone. Excellent location with the Hakone Open Air Museum is a short distance and the Hakone Cable Car and Ropeway less than five minutes away from the hotel.

Modern & mountainous: Hakone Ginyu. This modern Ryokan is built on the side of a mountain and all guest rooms have views of Hakone Mountain. There are 17 Japanese-style and 3 Western-style guest rooms and all guest rooms have a private outdoor hot spring bath on the terrace. Perfect for a couple wanting privacy.

Bathing by starlight: Tenseien Ryokan. This large Ryokan Hotel has 105 Japanese-style rooms, and all rooms have their own private baths and toilets. There are four shared indoor hot spring baths at Tenseien (same gender only) and most of them are open 24 hours a day. The two shared outdoor hot spring baths have a view of Tenseien's surrounding Japanese garden. All meals are Japanese-style and they are served in the privacy of the guest rooms.

Delicious Places to Eat

Bath & bar: Tenzan Notemburo. A well known onsen with 3 good value restaurants offering different cuisine, they also run a free shuttle bus from Hakone-Yumoto station.

Small & chic: Chikuzen. A very good udon restaurant, serving a delightful range of noodle dishes.

Shushi in style: The Kikka-so Inn. This former Imperial Villa, was built in 1895 and is located across the route 1 from the Fujiya Hotel. The restaurant offers three traditional Japanese set menus, known as Kaiseki cuisine, in the traditional Japanese house.

Opposite page. Snow Festival in Odori Park, Sapporo.

Focus On...
Outdoors in Hokkaido

Hokkaido is the second largest, northernmost and least developed of Japan's four main islands. With its unspoiled nature, Hokkaido attracts many outdoor lovers, including skiers and snowboarders in the colder seasons and hikers, cyclists and campers from June to September.

Starting the second week in February every year the town of Sapporo turns into a snow museum with snow statues, ice sculptures, snow mazes and sledging. This internationall renowned 'Snow Festival' attracts to million visitors a year. Odori Park which serves as the main venue is located in the city center, and a space extending 1.5km transforms into a snow museum. International Square (Nishi 11 chome, Odori) becomes the stage for the International Snow Statue Contest and every year more than 10 teams compete from all over the world. As this is a park, you can drop by whenever you like. The lit-up snow statues are so beautiful. Moreover, the ice sculptures displayed at the Susukino Site, which is also a famous nightspot district, create a truly fantastic world. Here, you will discover unique works with Hokkaido delicacies such as crab, cuttlefish and salmon frozen inside the ice, which are fun to look at.

The Daisetsuzan National Park, the largest national park in Japan is ideal if you want to immerse yourselves in nature on your honeymoon. It includes lakes, forests, volcanoes, several mountain groups, gorges, hot springs and remote mountain villages. The park is ideal for skiing, hiking, cycling, diving and golf. It has active volcanoes, beautiful alpine lakes and flowers, a 7 tier waterfall, free huts to sleep in, lots of wildlife (including bears), relaxing natural hot springs and challenging back country wilderness. From early May to mid October it is possible to hike without special gear in most places; from late September, it starts to snow in Daisetsu-zan, be extra prepared for possible snow and minus temperatures. That said, watching the change from fall to winter is one of the most enchanting times to see Daisetsu-zan National Park.

Stylish Essentials

General Information

Japan National Tourist Organisation
10th Floor, Tokyo Kotsu Kaikan Bldg, 2-10-1, Yurakucho,
Chiyoda Ward,
Tokyo 100-0006
www.jnto.go.jp
T. +81 (0) 3 3201 3331
Open: 9.00–17.00 daily

Airlines

ANA (All Nippon Airlines)
www.fly-ana.com
T. 0870 837 8811 (UK reservations)

British Airways
www.ba.com
T. 0844 493 0 787
(UK reservations & enquiries)

Cathay Pacific
www.cathaypacific.com
T. 020 8834-8888 (UK reservations)

JAL (Japan Airlines)
www.jal.com
T. 0845 7 747 700
(UK reservation & information)

Trains

Japan Rail Pass
www.japanrailpass.net

Tokyo

Imperial Household Agency
www.kunaicho.go.jp
(Japanese & English)
E. information@kunaicho.go.jp
(application for imperial palace visit)

La Forêt
1-11-6 Jingumae, Tokyo Shibuya-ku. Just off Harajuku's main intersection of Omotesando Dori and Meiji Dori
T. +81 (0) 3 3475 0411
Open: 11.00–20.00

Oriental Bazaar
5-9-13 Jingu-mae, Harajuku
T. +81 (0) 3 3400 3933
Open: 9.30–18.30 daily

Togo Shrine Flea Market
A Quaint Flea Market
1-5-3 Jingu-mae
Togo Shrine, Harajuku
T. +81 (0) 3 3425 7965
Open: 5.00–15.00 weekends

Department Stores

Matsuya Department Store
T. +81 (0) 3 3567 1211

Mikimono (The famous pearls store)
T. +81 (0) 3 3591 5001

Mitsukoshi Department Store
T. +81 (0) 3 3562 1111

Seibu Department store
T. +81 (0) 3 3286 0111

Wako store
(Good places to find Seiko watches)
T. +81 (0) 3 3562 2111

Isetan department store
T. +81 (0) 3 3352 1111

Kinokuniya bookstore
T. +81 (0) 3 3354 0131

Takashimaya Times Square
T. +81 (0) 3 5361 1122

Yodobashi Camera
in front of the Shinjuku station.
T. +81 (0) 3 3346 1010

Gas Panic (bar)
3-10-5, Roppongi Minato-ku,
T.+81 (0) 334 0270 54

Finger (a stylish hangout)
The B Roppongi Hotel
3-9-8 Roppongi, Minato-ku,

Keio Plaza Hotel (Karaoke)
Shinjuku
www.keioplaza.com

Lovenet (Karaoke)
Hotel Ibis 3F & 4F, 7-14-4 Roppongi, Minato-ku
www.ibis-hotel.com/en.html

P&A Plaza
1-17-9 Shibuya-ku, Dogenzaka,
www.paplaza.com
T. +81 (0) 3 3780 5211

Park Hyatt
3-7-1 2 Nishi-Shinjuku,
Shinjuku
www.parkhyatttokyo.com
T. +81 (0) 3 5322 1234

Mandarin Oriental
2-1-1 Nihonbashi Muromachi
Chuo-ku
www.mandarinoriental.com/tokyo/
T. +81 (0) 33270 8800

Robataya
Roppongi Hills, Yachiyo Building on Gaien Street
T. +81 (0) 3 3408 9674
Open:

Kyubei
8-7-6 Ginza, Chuo-ku
Ginza line to Shimbashi
T. + 81 (0) 3 3571 6523
Open: 11.30–14.00 & 13.00– 22.00

Tatou Tokyo
7-6-2 Roppongi, Minato-ku
T. +81 (0) 3 5411 2996
Open Tue-Fri 18.00–23.00
closed Mon

Kyoto

Wak Japan - Cultural Experiences
506-412 Iseya-cho, Kawaramachi
Marutamachi sagaru,
Kamigyo-ku, Kyoto, Japan 602-0873
www.wakjapan.com
T. +81 (0) 75 212 9993
E. wak@wakjapan.com

Gion Corner Theatre
Yasaka Hall Shijo-sagaru Hanami-koji
Higashiyama-ku, Kyoto
T. + 81 (0) 75 561 1119
Open: 19.00 and 20.00

Yoshimine-Dera Temple
1372 Oshio Ohanano Nishikyo-ku
www.yoshiminedera.com.
T. +81 (0) 75 331 0020
Open: 8.00–17.00
Access: 20min by taxi from Hamkyu Nagaoka-tenjin Station

Heian Shrine & Gardens
Open: 6:00–17:30 (slightly longer/ shorter in summer/winter)

Kyoto Handicraft Centre (selling arts, crafts and woodblock prints)
Shijo-dori-Higashioji
T. +81 (0) 561 9660
Open: 11.00–19.00

Arashima Park
Saga Ukyo-ku and Arashiyama Saikyo-ku Kyoto-shi
T. +81 (0) 75 701 0101
Access: 15 minutes on foot from JR SagaArashiyama station
5 minutes on foot from Keihuku and Hankyu Arashiyama station

Yoshikawa Inn
Tominokoji, Oike-sagaru, Nakagyo-ku, Kyoto
www.kyoto-yoshikawa.co.jp
T. +81 (0) 75 221 5544

Hiiragiya Ryokan
Nakahakusancho, Fuyacho Anekoji-agaru, Nakagyo-ku,
Kyoto 604-8094
www.hiiragiya.co.jp
T. +81 (0) 75 221 1136

Tawaraya Inn
Oike-Sagaru, Fuyacho, Nakagyo-ku, Central Kyoto
T. +81 (0) 75 211 5566

Friandise Imadegawa
Kawabata Imadegawa Higashi-Iru, Sakyo-Ku, Kyoto-city
T. +81 (0) 75 724 1172
Open: 7.00–19.00 daily

Ponto-Cho Uan
Gion Shirakawa Nawate Higashi iru,
T. +81 (0) 75 221 2269
Open: 11.30–22.00 closed Thursday

Hyotei
35 Kusakawa-cho, Nanzenji
Sakyo-ku, Kyoto 606-8437
www.hyotei.co.jp
T. +81 (0) 75 771 4116
Open: 11.00–21.00 daily

Hakone

Hakone Begonia Garden
www.hakone-begoniaen.com

Tenzan
Kanagawa prefecture Ashigarashimo-gun Hakone-cho Yumoto-tyaya 208
T. +81 (0) 460 6 4126
Short walk from "Oku-Yumoto Iriguchi" bus stop (5 minutes, 220 Yen from Yumoto Station along the Old Tokaido)
Open: 9.00–22.00 daily

Rakuyujurin Shizenkan
5 minute walk from "Hotel-mae" bus stop and the Fujiya Hotel or a 10 minute walk from Miyanoshita Station.
T. +81 (0) 460 82 0265
Open: 10.00–20.00 daily closed on Wednesdays

Yunessun Hot Springs Amusement Park
1297 Ninotaira Hakone-machi
Ashigarashimo-gun Kanagawa-ken
www.yunessun.com
T. +81 (0) 4602 4126

Mount Fuji Climbing Guides
(pilgrimage and expeditions)
www.fujimountainguides.com
T. +81 (0) 90 6477 7438

Tenseien Ryokan
682 Yumoto Hakone-machi
Ashigarashimo-gun
Kanagawa-ken
www.tenseien.co.jp

Gora Kadan
1300 Gora, Hakone,
Ashigarashimogun
Hakone 250-0408
www.gorakadan.com
T. +81 (0) 46082 3331
E. info@gorakadan.com

Hakone Ginyu
100-1 Miyanoshita Hakone-machi
Ashigarashimo-gun
Kanagawa-ken
www.hakoneginyu.co.jp
T. +81 (0) 250 0404

The Kikka-so Inn
Fujiya Hotel
T. +81 (0) 460 82 2211

Hokkaido

Sapporo Snow Festival
Odori Site, Susukino Site, Satorando Site in Sapporo
When: For 7 days, starting in the second week of February

Daisetsuzan National Park
T. +81 (0) 166 924 378
Transport: bus: to the park interior from Asahikawa, Furano, Biei, Kamikawa, Kitami & Obihiro

Tenzan Notemburo
Hakone machi; Ashigara Shimo-gun; Kanagawa Prefecture, 208 Yumoto Chay;
www.tenzan.jp
T. +81 (0) 11 81 460 86 4126

The Fujiya Hotel
359 Miyanoshita, Hakone-machi,
Kanagawa-ken 250-0404,
T. +81 (0) 460 82 2211(Ext. 638)
Open: 12.00–14.00 & 18.00–20.30

View of Longitude 131 and Ayers Rock, courtesy of Voyagers.

AUSTRALIA

New South Wales | Queensland |
Western Australia | Uluru |

AUSTRALIA

Why is this place so special?

Australia has come a long way since the days when Captain Cook stumbled ashore to find an Aboriginal way of life that went back some 40,000 years in 1770. Australia should really be divided into 'modern Australia' and 'indigenous Australia', since there is a wealth of disparate elements that constitute this compelling country. Australia is an enormous country with much to offer the intrepid independent traveller. Wonderful scenery, sandy beaches, slick cities, mysterious indigenous tribes and fabulous food and drink. Australia has become ever more popular over recent years due to increased internal flight routes and around-the-world fares serving the major cities, making it quite economical to get to and travel around. The fact that Australia is also English speaking makes it a popular destination for first-time backpackers.

Australia is a very large country made up of six states — New South Wales, Queensland, Victoria, South Australia, Western Australia and Tasmania — and two territories, the Northern Territory and the Australian Capital Territory. So it's difficult to know where to start, as each area offers different experiences. New South Wales boasts stunning mountain scenery, numerous vineyards and of course the cosmopolitan city Sydney; while Queensland offers incredible beaches, world class marine life and whilst most of Australia can offer outdoor activities, these are best experienced in the wonderful Western region. If you are lucky enough to have a month for your honeymoon then you might have time to explore all the regions. If you are thinking about combining your trip with a stopover then the South Pacific islands is only a short flight away.

Few countries can really boast as many different landscapes as Australia, and even fewer offer as much unoccupied open space. Australia is often called a "last frontier" country, so if you're seeking a pioneer-style getaway, you can find plenty of places to pitch a tent, light a barbeque and enjoy an undisturbed swim, or cast a line from a deserted beach.

From top. El Questro Homestead, Sydney Opera House, Blue Mountains.

Adventures come naturally in Australia – no other country has more scenic variety and few countries can rival Australian's zest for the great outdoors. Choose from vast outback plains, snow-capped mountains, wild rivers, forest-clad hills, plunging waterfalls, the scenic and massive Big Volcano National Park in New South Wales, miles of coastline, exotic tropical islands, the world's largest coral reef, rolling surf, and rock art that's 25,000 years old. Activities you can participate in include; bungee jumping, camel trekking, canoeing, rafting, hot-air ballooning, motorcycle touring, and theme-park visits.

Fast Facts

Capital: Canberra.

Location: Australia is the smallest continent in the world and the only continent occupied by a single country. Lying southeast of Asia, it is bound by the Pacific Ocean to the east, the Coral Sea to the northeast, the Timor Sea to the northwest, the Indian Ocean to the west and the Tasman Sea to the southeast.

Population: 21.2 million.

Religion: Catholic 26.4%, Anglican 20.5%, other Christian 20.5%, Buddhist 1.9%, Muslim 1.5%, other/unspecified 29.2%.

Languages: The official language is English, although Aboriginal and other ethnic languages are also spoken.

Opposite page from top. Three Sisters. Sydney Harbour Bridge. Petersons Winery in the Hunter Valley. Aussie barbeque.

Getting there and exploring around

Virtually all visitors arrive to Australia by air. The main international airports are Sydney, Melbourne and Brisbane, followed by Perth, Adelaide, Hobart, Darwin and Cairns. There are plenty of connections to Asia, Europe and the USA, but Australia's remoteness makes flights relatively expensive and long. It's often better value to purchase an 'around-the-world' ticket and stop off at different points on the out-bound and in-bound journeys. Many flights are heavily booked, so make plans well in advance, especially during the Christmas period when flight prices are at their highest.

Getting around Australia is convenient by air, but train is becoming increasingly popular. The classical and luxurious Ghan and Indian Pacifica trains can take you east to west (and vice versa) and north to south, they can be pricier than normal trains but the luxury and comfort is perhaps worth the expense, especially if you are on your honeymoon. Getting to Brisbane from Sydney is easy by travelling with CountryLink trains, you can buy a first class ticket on the overnight sleeper train including a warm breakfast which is good value for money.

Driving around Australia can be fairly easy, especially around major cities such as Sydney, allowing flexibility to visit the outskirts of towns and regions independently. Some areas (i.e. Uluru National Park) require special permits to enter, so please check with the local ranger beforehand.

Best time of year to visit

Australia is in the southern hemisphere and the seasons are opposite to those in Europe and North America. There are two climatic zones: the tropical zone (in the north above the Tropic of Capricorn) and the temperate zone. The tropical zone (consisting of 40 per cent of Australia) has two seasons, summer 'wet' and winter 'dry', while the temperate zone has all four seasons. Australia can experience hurricanes and cyclones on both coasts mainly on the northeast and northwest while droughts are also quite common.

Spring to summer (November to March) is warm or hot everywhere, tropical in the north, and warm to hot, with mild nights, in the south.

Autumn to winter (April to October) Northern and central Australia has clear warm days, cool nights; the south has cool days with occasional rain but still plenty of sun. Snow is totally confined to mountainous regions of the southeast.

Festivals and events do take place throughout the year, but notably during the summer time (January & February) the Mardi Gras in Sydney and the Sydney festival are highlights. During May, June & July there are a variety of food & wine festivals throughout the country.

? Must know before you go

Humour. When in the company of friends, it's not uncommon for Australians to 'take the mick' out of each other – usually a jovial exchange of mocking and putting down between friends and family. Modesty is considered a virtue in Australia, and this sort of exchange is only meant in jest, with no real weight behind any accusations. The more they 'take the mick' out of you generally speaking the more they like you.

Meeting & greeting. The Australian way of communicating is quite forthcoming and direct, and perhaps a little brash in contrast to their South Asian neighbours. Don't mistake this sort of approach for rudeness, as Australians are renowned straight talkers, yet relaxed and informal with it.

Socialising & shouting. Australians love their beer and wine. Beer is the most common tipple and it's considered good etiquette to buy a round of drinks. The colloquialism used for this is known as 'shouting a round'. No physical shouting is actually required, unless of course you find yourself in a noisy bar! Not buying a round of drinks will render you stingy and cheap in the eyes of locals. Australians are renowned for their love of barbeques. It almost goes without saying that you should bring your own beer, and any leftovers should be left to the host or hostess.

Highlights

Dine & indulge. Dine out on splendid seafood in one of Sydney's top notch restaurants, and indulge in the endless list of wines.

Beach bum. Don your 'sunnies' and 'cossie' on a beach in Queensland and explore the impressive underwater world on a diving trip to the Great Barrier Reef.

Outback action. Explore Western Australia's Bungle Bungle Range and the rocky landscapes of Karijini National Park.

Culture Vulture. Explore the ancient Aboriginal land at Uluru and wake up with a view of Ayres rock on the horizon.

Tip for the Trip

"If you buy souvenirs, it's sometimes easier and cheaper to pack a box and send them home via freight. Check out the local DHL or Post Office."

Jill

Opposite page. Lovedale, Hunter Valley.

Adventure: Gastronomy **Destination:** New South Wales

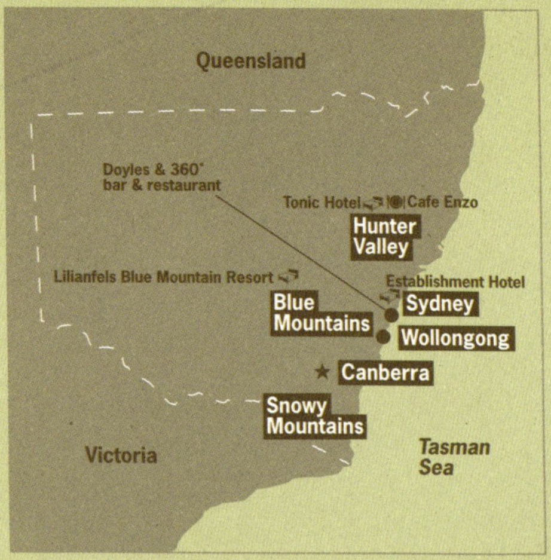

Regional Information

Some of Australia's most historic country towns dot this region. These quintessentially Australian settlements, founded by gold miners, graziers and farmers and chosen by artists for their special light, are loved by visitors today for their old-world general stores and friendly country pubs. Pioneering history, cultural events, museums, galleries, two World Heritage listed areas, the second oldest national park in the world, 40 national parks and reserves and fabulous food and wine are plentiful in this region. There is enough to keep any visitor occupied for at least a couple of weeks. If Sydney is your first stop then spend a few days exploring the city's highlights before heading to the outer regions.

As a city, Sydney began more than 200 years ago as a settlement for British convicts. Today it's a dynamic, thriving city of more than 3 million people, and the country's largest and densest population. The view of the harbour is dominated by the magnificent Opera House, and the waters are filled with ferries and boats of all shapes and sizes. Harbourside locations, the world's second largest seafood market and a bounty of fresh produce, grown locally, continue to inspire Sydney's most dynamic chefs. Hot new trends emerging right now are 'tasting menus' which allow you try small-sized servings in a multi-course meal and spectacularly creative desserts. Some of the desserts emerging from Sydney's kitchens are so fabulous you could frame them. Sydney is a hot destination for foodies, with flavours and venues to suit all budgets and palates. There's incomparable seafood, a rich multicultural dining experience and world-beating restaurants. Couples will find it difficult to decide on where to dine; from rooftop skyline restaurants to small fish & chip shops Sydney has an incredible variety.

Adventure: Gastronomy
Destination: New South Wales

Sydney's inner precincts are divided up into 19 areas. The Rocks and Circular Quay are good locations for lively evenings, boutique shops, galleries and walks. If you have the stomach for heights, one of the most incredible experiences is climbing the Sydney Harbour Bridge especially at twighlight as the sun sets over the Opera house (the first wedding there was recently conducted). The Rocks market at weekends is a lively spot full of local artisans selling fashion and farmers selling fresh produce. It has recently been revitalised (in 2008) to allow more space and stalls.

Regions close to Sydney include the Blue Mountains, Hawkesbury River, Central Coast, The Hunter, Blue Mountains, Illawarra, Port Stephens and Southern Highlands are all within a two-and-a-half-hour drive of Sydney. It's relatively easy to hire a car and head out, stopping off where you can, but there are several companies that do offer excellent small group tours to these areas, if you don't feel confident enough to drive.

The Hunter Valley is the birthplace of the commercial wine industry in Australia and is the most visited of all of the wine regions. More than 120 cellar doors make the Hunter's seven sub-regions irresistible to the wine lover. And while age-old traditions and respect for the discipline of quality-not-quantity remain the hallmark of Hunter winemaking, a vibrant contemporary food scene has grown up around it. Chocolate & cheese shops and olives, the universal companion to grapes - are produced in all their manifestations from oils to tapenades, and local seafood, meats, poultry and cheeses inspire the creativity of chefs in the region.

All this is supported by an infinite choice of accommodation options (especially quaint Lovedale) treks and tours, galleries and golf courses, rejuvenation spas and relaxation retreats. The Hunter wine and food fair in May attracts the regions best gourmet food producers and the Hunter Harvest festival in March and April celebrates the ancient ritual of harvest. There are plenty of guided tours around the area, leaving you free to enjoy wine tasting; you can even drift over the vineyards on a hot air balloon which is a lovely romantic experience.

Below from left. Establishment, Sydney. Doyles fish and chips.

Stylish Places to Stay

Luxury & romance: Lilianfels Blue Mountains Resort & Spa. Another Orient Express property with stunning views of the Blue Mountains. They offer 'La vie en Rose' romantic packages for couples which includes a bottle of champagne and romantic 3 course dinner. Fabulous for a night or two of luxury and pampering.

Hip & chic: Establishment Hotel. Located in central Sydney a short walk from the Circular Quay and the Opera house, this is one of the cool 'hip' places to be seen in Sydney. They boast a celebrity guest list as long as your arm and 'Tank bar' is one of Sydney's hottest nightspots. Book one of the two penthouses, with a bathroom as big as a house, for a night of luxury.

Homemade & homely: Hotel Tonic, Lovedale. Gorgeous, funky, chic cabins set in the Hunter valley countryside; with brilliant views of the vineyards and if you are lucky you might spot the odd kangaroo jumping over your balcony. The owners are very welcoming, helpful and can organise trips for you, there is also a lovely communal area where you can chat to other travellers. Prices include a homemade breakfast.

Delicious Places to Eat

Fish & fun: Doyles @ Watson bay. A fabulous find for the best fish & chips in the area. Catch a boat from Sydney's Circular Quay and dine overlooking the bay. Perfect for Sunday lunch, but book ahead as this place is packed with locals.

Charming & chic: Café Enzo, Hunter Valley. A lovely cosy restaurant with roaring fires in the winter and a garden patio for the summer. It's set in a quiet courtyard, serving home-made lunches with local wines.

City escape: 360˚ Bar & Restaurant. A revolving floor with stunning 360 degree views over the city. This is Australia's highest restaurant. The amazing night-time view gives it a tourist trap reputation, but this sky-high restaurant offers very fine dining indeed.

Oppostie page. Top. Great Barrier Reef, courtesy of Dreamstime. **Bottom.** Whitsunday Island Sailing, courtesy of Dreamstime.

Adventure: Beach
Destination: Queensland

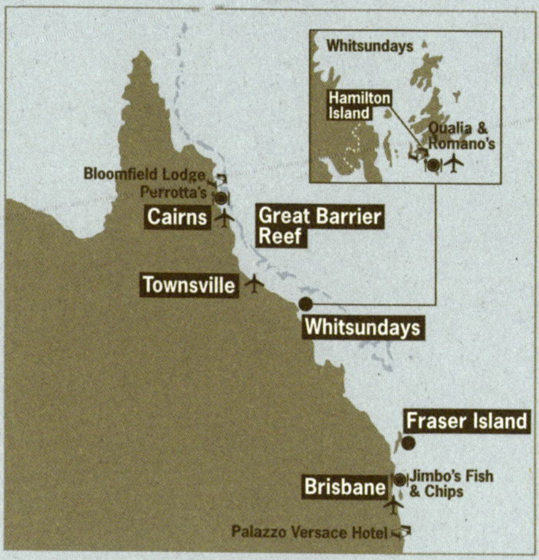

Regional Information

Pristine beaches, tropical islands and lush rainforests make Queensland the ultimate beach and outdoor honeymoon destination. Known as Australia's 'Sunshine State', Queensland offers an abundance of diverse experiences from chilling out on a beach, learning to surf and exploring the underwater world. The climate is usually warm year-round (the further north you travel the hotter it is) which makes it popular in summer and winter.

Brisbane is the state's capital city, a city full of energy, style, arts and culture. The Brisbane River snakes through the metropolis and is peppered with alfresco dining options. By night, the city comes alive with vibrant bars and live music venues to keep you entertained into the early hours of the morning. Brisbane is also home to the famous 'Surfers Paradise' beach which stretches for miles and is a good base to explore the Gold Coast and Sunshine Coast, which is only an hour away by road. Both coastal regions offer stunning beaches. Head further north to swim in the freshwater lakes of Fraser Island, the largest sand island in the world, and just one of Queensland's five World Heritage listed areas.

With 36,735km (22,826 miles) of coastline, Australia provides outstanding opportunities for watersports, particularly diving and snorkelling. The tropical waters along the 2500km (1500 miles) of the Great Barrier Reef and its multitude of tiny islands form one of the world's best-known diving locations. Requirements for dive courses (which are widely available) vary from state to state; something to consider if you are taking a 'familymoon', beginners must be at least 12 years old and all divers must have a medical certificate of fitness in accordance with Australian standards.

Adventure: Beach
Destination: Queensland

To obtain the basic scuba diving qualification, visitors can participate in either a one-week full-time course or a two-week part-time course; tailor-made courses are also available. Certified divers must be able to produce their international certification card and log book for solo dives, unless they participate in fully supervised dives with a professional. One of the best ways to explore unchartered dive sites is to stay on a 'live-aboard' for a few nights. There are plenty of companies that offer different 'live-aboard' experiences from luxury to very basic. It's a good way to get qualified quickly in an intense environment, or if your other half doesn't fancy it, they can enjoy some snorkelling or relax on the boat.

The Whitsunday Coast and Islands are a very special part of Australia. Centrally located on the Queensland Coast 150km north of Mackay and 300km south of Townsville yet right in the heart of the World Heritage listed Great Barrier Reef. Flights depart from most cities daily, with direct access to Hamilton Island in the Whitsundays or Whitsunday Coast Airport 45 minutes from Airlie Beach. A romantic way to explore the Whitsundays is by boat, you can easily charter a sailing yacht or motorboat for the day from a variety of local companies. Airlie Beach is the main departure point for vessels heading to the Whitsunday Island Group, and therefore it has a huge population of charter vessels, itinerant yachties, and holidaymakers keen on sailing in what has been described as one of the world's most beautiful cruising areas.

The beach at Airlie faces the islands to the north. Mt. Rooper, Pioneer Point and the Mandalay Peninsula shield the waters here from the southeast winds. Therefore, Airlie Beach is very protected and calm - perfect for relaxing sun-soaking afternoon. Surfing conditions in these regions are excellent, which is why several international surf tournaments are held here every year. The Whitsunday Islands are composed of 74 Isles, the most notable being Daydream Island, Hamilton Island, Hayman Island, Hook Island, Lindeman Island, Long Island and South Molle. These islands are dominated by resorts but the remaining 67 islands which form part of the Great Barrier Reef Marine Park are controlled by National Park Authorities. Visiting these islands is permissible by chartered boats or private yachts; however it is necessary to obtain a camping permit if you intend to stay overnight. The most pristine beach in the Whitsunday Island Group is Whitehaven Beach. This 6 kilometre beach is famous for it's pure white sand and feeling of remoteness. No human infrastructure can be seen from the beach - only the water gently lapping at the white sand and the endless expanse of the Pacific Ocean to the east.

Below left. Qualia, Winward Daybed.
Right. Jimbo's Seafood, Brisbane

Stylish Places to Stay

Deluxe charm: Qualia. Just a stone's throw off the Queensland coast, Qualia sits on Hamilton Island. Each pavilion is equipped with the latest technology and highest standard of accessories (eg Villeroy and Boch, icemaking machine, etc) and you get your own golf buggy to drive yourself around the island.

Indulge in style: Palazzo Versace. Indulge in the sensual elegance of classical design in one of Australia's most luxurious hotel. Typical Versace, its flamboyant, its over the top and its incredibly luxurious. Sun yourself at the lagoon pool area, hire a boat on the private marina, or shop in the 'Versace' store for anything and everything carrying the famous brand.

Rainforest retreat: Bloomfield Lodge. Located north of Cairns, this honeymoon retreat has received rave reviews and it's easy to see why. Take a private picnic on the beach with a bottle of champagne or laze on the stunning jetty. They also organise rainforest walks for those with itchy feet. Note: there is a 4-night minimum stay

Delicious Places to Eat

Fish picnic: Jimbo's Fish 'N' Chips. Perhaps the best fish and chips you'll ever eat, this laid back restaurant is more like a fish market, pick your fish, select your cooking method and sit on a picnic table outside and indulge.

Stylish seafood: Romano's Italian Restaurant. A lovely romantic spot for a upmarket Italian treat. Overlooking the Hamilton Island marina and serving traditional Italian favourites such as pasta and local seafood like Spring Bay mussels.

Café chic: Perrotta's. Located in Cairns, the locals flock here for brunch and lunch, particularly on weekends and you can team it with a visit to the Cairns Regional Art Gallery (the café is just outside).

Opposite page. **Top.** Bungle Bungles, courtesy of Dreamstime. **Bottom.** The Pinnacles Desert, courtesy of Dreamstime.

Adventure: Action
Destination: Western Australia

Regional Information

Fishing, kayaking, scuba diving, sky diving, hiking, surfing… tired yet? Couples with a lust for adventures will rarely be short of action in Western Australia. The many National Parks are scattered across this region, all with different propositions; within an hour from Perth, the Serpentine National Park is a picturesque park in a scenic cleft of the ancient Darling Scarp, with wonderful rock filled pools and cascading waterfalls, which is a perfect escape from the bustling city.

Nambung National Park is home of the mystical Pinnacles Desert, where thousands of limestone pillars rise up to three and a half metres tall from the shifting yellow sands. These extraordinary ancient rock formations that make up the Pinnacles are located about a three-hour drive north of Perth near the coastal town of Cervantes. Regarded as one of Australia's most unique landscapes, the incredible limestone spiers rise eerily out of the sand, some several metres tall. You can get up-close to the Pinnacles on a scenic drive and walk trail that includes an amazing lookout over the Nambung National Park. It's believed the Pinnacles were created millions of years ago as seashells were broken down into sand and then eroded by water and wind. The best time to visit is between August and October when the wildflowers are in bloom, and although you can't actually stay in the national park you can visit on a day tour either with a group, or go it alone.

At the Leeuwin-Naturaliste National Park, you can often spot migrating humpback and southern whales from the craggy sea cliffs and windswept granite headlands. There's a towering karri forest and two self-guided caves to explore as well. It's located to the Eastern boundary, along the sealed Yallingup/Augusta Caves Road and access to the Southern portion is by sealed Bussell Highway to Augusta. Within the Park all two wheel drive roads are gravel & four wheel tracks are rough. There is also a bus service to and from Perth if you don't fancy the drive.

Opposite page from top. Room at the Outram, courtesy of Wyndham Vacation Resorts. Leeuwin Estate Restaurant Veranda.

Adventure: Action **Destination:** Western Australia

The Yanchep National Park (located only 45 minutes north of Perth) is amongst the oldest National Parks in Western Australia. Its unique fauna and flora as well as its rich Aboriginal and European Heritage make this an interesting spot for those who enjoy nature, and for wildlife lovers as there is a Koala colony. There are six or seven good bush walks ranging from easy to hard through the woodlands and caves, and maps are available from the visitors centre for those who want to explore alone.

A must see is the World Heritage listed Purnululu National Park and the Bungle Bungle range, as its one of the most fascinating geological landmarks in Western Australia. From an aircraft, the Bungle Bungle Range is an imposing sight. The orange and black stripes across the beehive-like mounds, encased in a skin of silica and algae, are clearly visible as you approach from the south. As you sweep further over the range a hidden world of gorges and pools is revealed, with fan palms clinging precariously to walls and crevices within the rocks.

Although the Bungle Bungle Range was extensively used by Aboriginal people during the wet season, when plant and animal life was abundant, few Europeans knew of its existence until the mid-1980s. The area has been a National Park since 1987, and the park offers a remote wilderness experience. There are few facilities and no accommodation; visitors must carry in all food and water. Most visitors camp for several days so it is essential to be well equipped. You can camp at Walardi and Kurrajong campsites or alternatively you can four wheel drive to them and spend the day hiking, or take to the sky for an aerial view.

Perth and the surrounding area attract droves of surfers to its stunning beaches each year, both professional and beginners. Western Australia has some of the best surf beaches. If you are looking for waves closer to the Perth region, there's Scarborough, Rottnest and Lancelin all within easy reach of the city.

With over 300 days of sunshine per year, the most for any city in Australia, Perth is the perfect city to plan sky-diving. The premier sky-dive company operating out of Perth is Sky-Dive Express, and with over 2,500 people leaping out of their fleet of planes each year, its popular but it's not for the fainthearted.

Western Australia also has the largest shore-line of any state in Australia, and the diving is considered some of the best in the world; whether it be with the Whale Sharks off Ningaloo Reef, exploring the caves and reefs of Rottnest Island just 45 minutes from Perth, or even diving the eerie HMS Swan wreck near Busselton, Western Australia boasts a range of dive sites that rival the Great Barrier Reef. Sea kayaking is also another popular activity from Penguin Island near to Perth to Ningaloo Reef near Exmouth, or even the winter warmth of Cable Beach in Broome, kayaking is a unique way to find adventure along the contrasting coastlines of the state, and a lovely activity to do as a couple.

Stylish Places to Stay

Chic & sleek: The Outram. Modern, minimalist and custom-built from scratch on a quiet street in west Perth, The Outram impresses with its sleek French design and townhouse chic. Malcolm and Pauline Tew's ideal boutique hotel was inspired by travels in Europe, and it really stands out from the city's anodyne commercial hotels. Only 18 rooms so book early especially during the peak season.

Antique charm: El Questro Homestead. An exclusive retreat cantilevered over the magnificent Chamberlain River, where guests will enjoy absolute luxury, contrasted by the rugged Kimberley landscape. Decorated with artifacts and antiques collected from Indonesia and tropical Australia, the Homestead boasts a swimming pool, spa and tennis court set in lush, tropical gardens. Book a gourmet picnic by helicopter for a special treat.

Secluded chic: Yallingup Luxury Retreat. Each of the five villas is tucked away behind limestone walls and landscaped Australian native gardens for total seclusion and privacy. Take advantage of the private chef - beautiful food cooked and served in your villa and the chef even cleans up completely!

Delicious Places to Eat

Beer & bistro: Sail & Anchor. Enjoy some of the best modern Australian pub food in Fremantle at the courtyard cafe that is built around the legendary Sail & Anchor brewery. This unique café offers alfresco dining all year round but in winter it is warm and snug with gas heaters on and the room closed.

Gorgeous & glamorous: Opus at The Richardson. Opus at The Richardson is one of Perth's most glamorous dining experiences, providing an opulent, luxurious backdrop for fine dining in west Perth. Opus boasts its own Wine Annex; the raised semi-private section of the restaurant displays a library of fine wines against a natural stone backdrop - ideal for wine tastings. Dress up for dining as this place is glam.

Wine & dine: Leeuwin Estate (Winery). Famous for their annual outdoor concerts, Leeuwin Estate is the epitome of fine food and wine. In a setting guaranteed to take your breath a way (with cozy interior and open log fires), its award winning restaurant is perfect for a romantic evening.

Opposite page. Longitude 131.

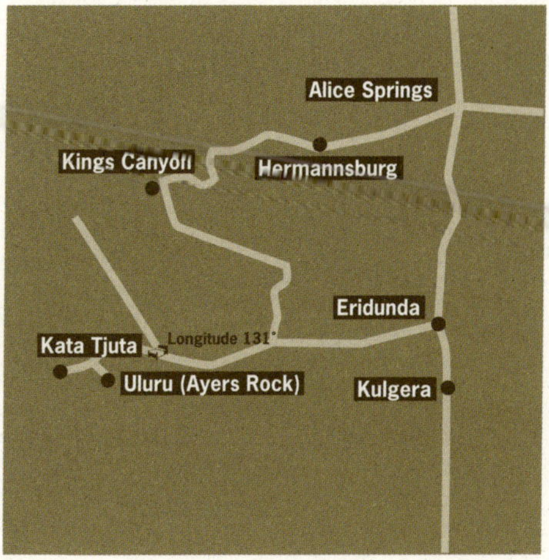

Focus On...
Culture in Uluru

Uluru, also referred to as Ayers Rock, is a large sandstone rock formation in the southern part of the Northern Territory, central Australia. It is one of Australia's most recognized icons, and naturally one of Australia's most visited attractions, although the best time to visit is in the Autumn and Winter when there are less flies (which become extremely annoying during the summer months) and its cooler, making it pleasant to hike around. Depending on the time of day and the atmospheric conditions, the rock can dramatically change colour, anything from blue to violet to glowing red. Many avid photographers set up for days to record the many changing colours of Uluru.

Uluru lies 335 km (208 miles) south west of the nearest large town, Alice Springs; 450 km (280 miles) by road. Kata Tjuta (The Olgas) and Uluru are the two major features of the Uluru - Kata Tjuta National Park. Uluru is sacred to the Pitjantjatjara and Yankunytjatjara, the Aboriginal people of the area, and is considered the cultural heart of the land. It has many springs, waterholes, rock caves and ancient paintings, dating back thousands of years. Today many Aboriginal people continue to paint and draw, and original artwork can be purchase from the Maruku arts & crafts centre.

Uluru is listed as a World Heritage Site, and you are encouraged not to climb the rock because of its sacred significance, though many tourists choose to ignore this advice and of course accidents do happen; out of respect the local Aboriginals go into a 'mourning period' of 3 months.

The most exclusive place to stay is Longitude 131, wonderful and luxurious pitched tents offer unspoilt views of Ayers Rock. The room rate includes daily sunrise and sunset trips to Ayers rock and Kata Tjuta, all meals (dining on a large table with other guests), return airport transfers and unlimited open bar.

ⓘ Stylish Essentials

General Information

Tourism Australia in the UK
Australia Center, Australia House,
6th Floor, Melbourne Place,
Strand, London WC2B 4LG, UK
www.australia.com
T. 020 7438 4601
(UK trade enquiries only).

Australian Wine & Beer information
PO Box 37, Mermaid Beach,
Queensland,
Australia 4218
www.australianwineandbeer.com
E. info@australianwineandbeer.com

Australian Official Tourist Travel
www.australia.com

Airlines

Qantas
www.qantas.com.au
T. 0845 7 747 767
(UK reservations line)
T. +44 208 600 4300
(Outside UK reservations)

Singapore Airlines
www.singaporeair.com
T. 0844 800 2380
(UK reservations line)

Virgin Blue
www.virginblue.com.au
T. +61 (0) 7 3295 2296 (Outside UK)

OneWorld (Around-the-world airfare)
www.oneworld.com

Trains

Rail Australia Alliance
Indian Pacifica & The Ghan & The Tilt Train
www.railaustralia.com.au
E. enquiries@railaustralia.com.au

CountryLink
www.countrylink.info
T. +61 (0) 2 132 232

New South Wales

General Information
www.visitnsw.com

Festivals & Events Guide
www.sydneyfestivals.com.au

The Rocks Market
Market located at the northern end of George Street
www.therocksmarket.com.au
Open: Sat & Sun 10.00–17.00

Sydney Harbour Bridge Climb
5 Cumberland Street,
The Rocks, Sydney
www.bridgeclimb.com
T. +61 (0) 2 8274 7777

Sydney Opera House
Box Office, GPO Box R239
Royal Exchange, Sydney NSW 1225
www.sydneyoperahouse.com
T. +61 (0) 9250 7111 (general enquiries)
Open: Tours 9.00–17.30

Hunter Valley Wine Tour
Sample some of the regions finest Shiraz.
www.allhunterwinetours.4t.com
Private Tours available contact Mike
E. ahwt@bigpond.net.au

Australian Eco Adventures
(Blue Moutain tours, Port Stephens, Sydney)
3/158 South Creek Rd, Cromer,
NSW 2099
www.ozeco.com.au
T. +61 (0) 2 9971-2402

Hot Air balloon rides
(Hunter Valley, Sydney, Gold Coast)
www.balloonaloft.com
T. +61 (0) 2 4991 1955
(NSW bookings)
E. balloons@balloonaloft.com

Lilianfels Blue Mountains resort
Lilianfels Avenue, Echo Point,
Katoomba
NSW, 2780
www.lilianfels.com.au
T. +61 (0) 2 4780 1200

Establishment Hotel
248-252 George St, Sydney
www.merivale.com
T. +61 (0) 2 9240 3100

Hotel Tonic
251 Talga Rd, Lovedale,
www.tonichotel.com.au
T. +61 (0) 2 4930 9999
E. stay@tonichotel.com.au

Doyles @ Watsons Bay
11 Marine Parade, Watsons Bay,
Sydney
www.doyles.com.au
T. +61 (02) 9337 2007
E. beach@doyles.com.au
Open 7 days, Lunch 12.00–15.00,
Dinner 18.00–21.00

Café Enzo's
Peppers Creek, Broke Road, Pokolbin
T. +61 (0) 4998 7233
Open: 7 days 9.00–17.00

360 bar & dining room
At Centrepoint, 100 Market Street
Sydney NSW 2000
www.360dining.com.au
T. +61 (0) 2 8223 3800
Open: Dinner 7 days. Open for Lunch Wed, Thurs, Fri, Sun.

Queensland

PADI
www.padi.com

Dive Directory
PO Box 5264, Cairns
Queensland 4870
T. +61 (0) 7 4046 7304
E. info@dive-australia.com

Surfing Australia
PO Box 1613, Kingscliff,
NSW 2487
www.surfingaustralia.com
T. +61 (0) 2 6674 9888

Sailing Whitsundays
www.sailingwhitsundays.com
T. +61 (0) 7 4946 5299

Qualia
www.qualia.com.au
T. +61 (0) 2 9433 3349
E. reservations@qualia.com.au

Bloomfield Lodge
Weary Bay
Po Box 966
Ayton, QLD 4032
www.bloomfieldlodge.com.au

Jimbo's Fish N Chips
123 Lae Dr, Runaway Bay, Brisbane
T. +61 (0) 7 5500 5777

Romano's Italian Restaurant
Marina Village, Harbourside, Hamilton Island, Queensland
T. +61 (0) 7 4946 8212
Open: every day except Tuesday

Perrotta's
Abbott and Shields sts, In Cairns
T. +61 (0) 7 4031 5899
Open: daily 8.30 till late

Western Australia

Outdoor Specialist
Unit 5/324 Orrong Road
Welshpool, Western Australia
www.adventureout.com.au
T. +61 (0) 8 9472 3919

Surfing Schools

Big Wave Surf (near Perth)
www.bigwavesurfingschool.com
T. +61 (0) 8 9524 7671

Adrift Surfing
Surf camps & safaris'
www.adriftsurfing.com

SkyDive Express
www.skydive.co.au
T. +61 (0) 8 9444 4199

The Outram
32 Outram Street, West Perth
www.wyndhamvrap.com.au
T. +61 (0) 8 9322 4888

El Questro Homestead
Via Gibb River Road, Kununurra, Western Australia, 6743
www.elquestrohomestead.com.au
T. +61 (0) 8 9169 1666

Yallingup Luxury Retreat
111 Marrinup Dr, Yallingup, WA 6282
www.yallingupluxuryretreat.com.au
T. +61 (0) 4 0097 5123

Sail & Anchor
64 South Terrace, Fremantle
WA 6160
www.sailandanchor.com.au
T. +61 (0) 8 93358433

Opus at The Richardson
32 Richardson Street
West Perth WA 6005
www.therichardson.com.au
T. +61 (0) 8 9217 8888

Leeuwin Estate (Winery)
Stevens Road
Margaret River WA 6285
www.leeuwinestate.co.au
T. +61 (0) 8 9759 0000
Open: Daily for lunch & Saturday evenings only

Uluru (Ayres Rock)

Maruku Arts
C.M.A. Ininti Store
Ayers Rock, NT 0872
Australia
www.maruku.com.au
T. +61 (0) 8 8956 2153
E. punu@maruku.com.au

Longitude 131
Uluru-Kata Tjuta National Park
www.longitude131.com.au
T. +61 (0) 2 9339 1040

Bora Bora, view from St Regis resort.

SOUTH PACIFIC

Fiji | French Polynesia | Cook Islands | Vanuata |

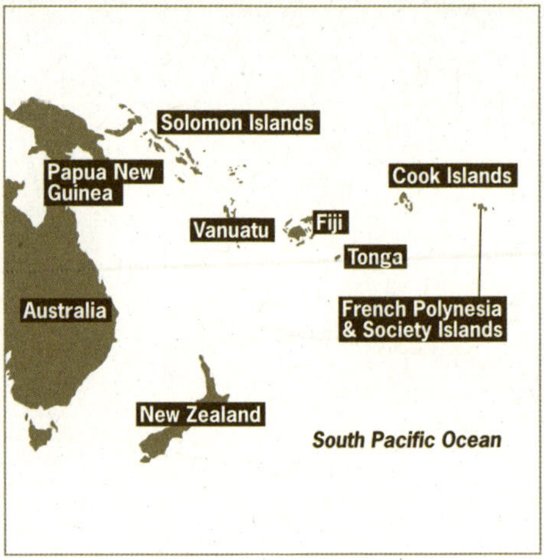

Why is this place so special?

The Pacific Ocean covers a third of the world's surface - it is a massive 64,500,000 square miles and most of this is ocean with only 500,000 square miles is land. Over 90% of this land is on the relatively large islands of Papua New Guinea, New Zealand and Australia. However, there are literally thousands more islands, many of which are mere coral atolls less than 5 metres above sea level that are unchartered and uninhabited.

The popular honeymoon destinations are the Cook Islands, Fiji, Vanuatu and French Polynesia, which attract the masses, but don't let that put you off. These islands are all unique and have their own special and individual allure. Each has carved out its own identity, yet each is fundamentally Polynesian. Sitting on the border between Polynesia and the Melanesian islands to the West, Fiji has its own distinctive culture blending elements from both areas. The Fijians also share their islands with East Indians, who add a starkly contrasting culture to the mix. Spending some time island hopping and perhaps including a stopover in New Zealand or Australia, will allow you to make the most of travelling across the other side of the globe.

There are three types of islands in the Pacific - volcanic, coral atolls and limestone islands. Samoa and New Zealand are stunning examples of extreme volcanic landscape; whilst the volcanic peaks are the visible islands, great chasms and massive marine mountains lie beneath the Pacific Ocean. Volcanic islands subside back into the sea, and erosions occurs causing deep lagoons such as Bora Bora in French Polynesia and Aitutaki in the Cook Islands. Over time, coral reefs and lagoons form around these new volcanic islands, like those witnessed in the Mamanuca Group in Fiji which makes them stunning dive locations, and over time the soft coral crushes into stunning white sand.

From top. Hammock in Bora Bora. Diving in the South Pacific. Coconut catching in Fiji.

The coral reefs also die to form limestone islands which have craggy coastlines but rocky interiors, and spectacular cliffs like those found in the Cook Island (Mangaia is believed to be the oldest island in the Pacific).

As a region, the South Pacific is filled with numerous outstanding attractions. These enchanting, beautiful islands have welcomed visitors for hundreds of years. From dreamy palm-fringed beaches and rugged volcanic peaks to dense rainforests with cascading waterfalls, have stirred the minds of many travellers. The islands of the South Pacific are essentially, pure paradise. Adventures for loved-up couples include diving or snorkelling among colourful marine life, venturing into the jungle on a bushwalk, visiting a traditional village or finding your own spot on the beach drinking sundowners.

Fast Facts

Capital: Suva (Fiji); Papeete (French Polynesia); Avarua (Cook Islands).

Location: The Pacific Ocean contains around 30,000 islands. Those lying south of the tropic of Cancer but excluding Australia are traditionally grouped into three divisions: Melanesia, Micronesia, and Polynesia.

Population: 853,445 (Fiji); 259,596 (French Polynesia); 18,700 (Cook Islands).

Religion: Christianity is the main religion of the South Pacific islands.

Languages: English & Bauan-Fijian (Fiji); French (French Polynesia); English (Cook Islands).

Opposite page from top. Cutting a coconut in Fiji. Fiji sunset. Sea anemone, Fiji.

Getting there and exploring around

Reaching the South Pacific islands by air can be pricey, so it is sometimes more economical to purchase an around-the-world air ticket (RTW), such as The Great Escapade or Star Alliance. This can also allow some flexibility with your itinerary, such as date and route changes, you can also stop off at other destinations like Auckland, Los Angeles, Sydney and Hawaii.

Collectively and with the addition of more South Pacific Airlines, several airlines have set a number of 'Pass products' that makes it easy for the traveller to plan an itinerary covering several island destinations. Air New Zealand has a South Pacific Airpass, which provides between 2 and 10 flight coupons for island hopping. Travel must begin in a South Pacific country, including Australia and New Zealand, and must conclude within 30 days. If you don't have an RTW ticket you could opt for this pass which might be more economical, although this does depend on the time of year you travel.

Depending on the carrier, the South Pacific has 4 airfare seasons: High season, is from December through to February. Mid-season covers March and April; a second mis-season runs from September to November. Low season from May to August (when the weather is at its finest on the islands), and fares can vary by as much as 25% depending on the season.

Once at the airport there are several ways to reach your 'island', the best and most exhilarating way is by 'sea-plane' which is usually an amphibious plane taking off the runway and landing on the sea. These are often privately chartered and can give you a great birds-eye view of all the atolls. Taking a private boat is also an option.

Best time of year to visit

Winter (May to October) is generally cooler, drier, and less humid throughout the region; this is the best time to go. Daytime high temperatures reach the delightful upper 70's (24°C-27°C) to low 80's (28°C-30°C) in French Polynesia, Samoa, and Fiji, with early morning lows in the high 60's (18°C-20°C). Rarotonga in the Cook Islands and Tongatapu in Tonga are farther from the equator and see cooler temperatures, with the highs in the 60's or low 70's (15°C-23°C). Wintertime nights can feel chilly in those islands.

The summer from November to April is warmer and more humid. Daytime highs climb into the upper 80's (30°C-33°C) throughout the islands, with night-time lows around 70°F (21°C). There maybe several days of rain at a time, but usually heavy rain showers are followed by periods of intense sunshine. July and August are the busiest times in the South Pacific, which is when Australians and New Zealanders visit the islands to escape the cold back home. It's also when residents of Tahiti head to their own outer islands, in keeping with the traditional July-August holidays in France.

Every country also has major celebrations, the annual Heiva Nui in French Polynesia, the King's Birthday in Tonga, and the week of Constitution Day in Rarotonga. These are the best times to see traditional dancing, arts, and sporting events. Be sure to make your reservations in advance, for hotel rooms and airline seats can be in short supply. The islands are also extraordinarily beautiful when there is a full moon so keep that in mind when planning your trip.

? Must know before you go

Shop around. Be sure to shop around all the airlines before flying to South Pacific, to see who has the best deals. Keep calling and checking the websites if no attractive fare is available at first; because wholesalers and groups often reserve blocks of low-cost seats in advance but release some of them near the date of departure. Occasionally a carrier will hold a last-minute sale to get rid of unused seats, so always ask for the lowest fare.

Hop around. Some of the islands are quite remote (i.e. the Yasawas in Fiji), this can make it difficult to explore independently, as many islands only have one resort, you won't have much choice in terms of eating out. It's a good idea to island hop, spending a couple of nights on each island in order to explore and make the most of your trip.

Importing/exporting. No fresh groceries can be brought into Cook Islands or Australia and New Zealand and your bags will be vigorously checked at customs for any 'banned or regulated' products such as wooden articles (without a certification), animal products or anything agricultural (even soil on your shoes!). If you are flying through, check with customs that your souvenirs won't be ceased on arrival.

Highlights

Shipwrecked survival. Explore the castaway beaches in Fiji, get shipwrecked for a day and learn to drink 'cava' in a typical Fijian ceremony.

Culture vulture. Immerse yourself in the culture of French Polynesia, observe the art of Tahitian tattoos and listen to vibrant music & dance.

Spa in style. Indulge in a relaxing and luxurious spa treatment in the Cook Islands and enjoy a day trip to beautiful Aitutaki on the stunning blue lagoon

Tricks of the tribes. Explore the shipwrecks, tribal culture and volcanic islands of Vanuatu.

Tip for the Trip

"Splash out on a surprise sea plane or helicopter flight to make the honeymoon extra special."

Carlo

Opposite page. Beach scene in Mamanucas.

Adventure: Beach
Destination: Fiji

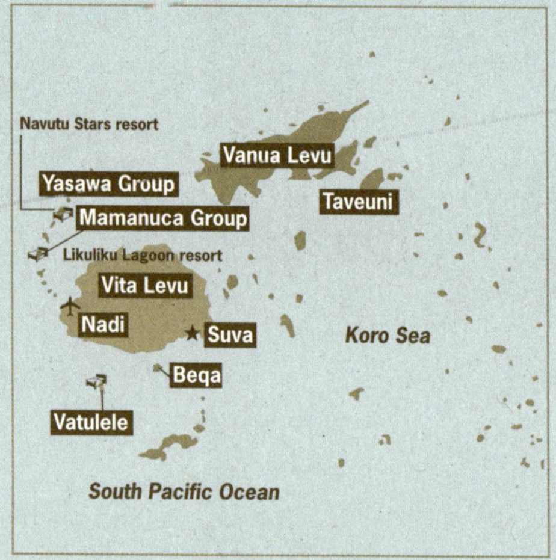

Regional Information

A day napping on a hammock with powder white sand beneath you, palm trees gently swaying outside your secluded 'bure' (beach bungalow); lazy days and sunsets with a cocktail in hand while watching the spectacular sunsets and dinner on the waters edge, promise a typical story book honeymoon. But Fiji is far more than just another sandy beach.

Fiji has the most fascinating mix of people in the South Pacific, extremely friendly, easygoing indigenous Fijians, who still live in traditional villages, and East Indians Fijians of Indian origin who settled in Fiji from the early 1900's. Indo Fijians are concentrated in the so-called 'Sugar Belt' and in cities and towns on the Northern and Western coast; their numbers are much scarcer in the south and inland areas. Although the contrasting Fijian-Indian cultures have resulted in some political unrest in the past, it is a calm and stunning country to visit.

The Fijian archipelago is located only a few hours from New Zealand and Australia so if you are visiting this side of the world, a trip over to Fiji to explore the 330 islands is a must. Because its international airport at Nadi is the region's major transportation hub, Fiji is a prime place with which to begin or end a trip to the South Pacific. In fact, more than twice as many people of every income bracket visit Fiji each year as it's one of the more affordable countries in the South pacific.

Fiji has something for everyone - from lying on some of the region's best beaches to diving on some of the world's most colourful reefs; cruising to intriguing outer islands to hiking into the mountainous interior. The best way to make the most of a trip here is to spend a week or two island hopping.

Island hopping is the most favourable way to experience Fiji, and an "Island Hop" ticket with Awesome Adventures or the 'Bula Pass' are economical ways to travel. Alternatively if you prefer to experience a variety of islands and want to know where you're heading then opt for one of the pre arranged 'Awesome Adventures' itineraries.

Independently the easiest way to travel between islands is by plane (and seaplane) with Fiji Air and Sun Air between them, servicing all of the island groups (Island Hoppers, Turtle Airways and Pacific Island Seaplanes fly some routes too). Ferries are inexpensive, frequent, reliable and very seaworthy, and rubbing shoulders with the local people while travelling between islands is a pleasant and interesting part of the Fiji experience. If you have more time then taking a ferry is ideal.

Unique and unspoilt, the islands of Fiji offer a thousand miles of pristine white sand beaches, fabulous coral gardens, swaying palm trees and amazing azure lagoons. This is the ideal place for a truly relaxing honeymoon. Set amongst deep blue waters with fringing coral reefs of turquoise and pastel green, the easily accessible and popular Mamanuca (pronounced Mamanutha) Islands or the untouched and idyllic Yasawa Islands offer you some of Fiji's finest beaches.

The Mamanuca Island's are close to Nadi, which make it more accessible. In early 2001, movie-goers worldwide got a taste of the rugged beauty of Fiji's Westernmost islands from Robert Zemeckis' blockbuster film Cast Away. The story revolves around a time-obsessed FedEx employee (Tom Hanks) who becomes stranded on an uninhabited tropical island after his plane goes down in the Pacific. At the time, concerns were raised that there might be a repeat of the damaging controversy surrounding the filming of 'The Beach' in Thailand, when Leonardo DiCaprio and 20th Century Fox were accused of inflicting serious environmental damage on Maya Beach in Krabi's Phi Phi Islands National Park. To avoid this, Zemeckis was careful to have veteran naturalist and author Dick Watling prepare an environmental code of conduct for the filming. Although no local Fijians actually appeared in Castaway, the film communicates the captivating and exotic Fijian scenery marvellously.

Adventure: Beach
Destination: Fiji

The Fiji archipelago has over 300 islands scattered across 200,000 square miles of ocean, so there is every chance a couple can experience a desert-island for a day at least. The filming mainly took place on tiny Monuriki Island, adjacent to Yanuya and between Matamanoa and Tokoriki, in the Mamanucas.

Monuriki is uninhabited, with unique flora and fauna, a picture postcard beach and secluded caves which can be experienced in a day trip from one of the neighbouring resorts. Pottery making is also abundant here, and you can watch the local women making vases and bowls in almost every Fijian community, one of the most welcoming is Yanuya, where the locals will almost certainly encourage you to drink a cup of spicy, local brew 'kava', made out of a root which has an alleged 'intoxicating' effect.

The majority of the other resorts are located in the Yasawa Island group offering beautiful white sand beaches and crystal clear lagoons with an amazing array of marine life - just perfect for snorkelling and diving. You'll also have the opportunity to experience true Fijian culture as many of the places you stay are owned and operated by the local Fijians who can accommodate you with an island tour including a visit to their nearby village and school. The closest of the Yasawa Islands is Kuata, which boasts high picturesque peaks with spectacular views. Naviti Island is the highest and largest in the group and has many long golden sand beaches as well as great snorkelling. Nacula Island is one of the furthest away and is home to four local villages, beautiful beaches and rugged hills, an ideal spot for exploring.

Up in Northern Fiji, Savusavu and Taveuni will transport you back in time to the Fiji of colonial coconut plantations. Between them lies the Somosomo Strait, home to the Great White Wall and its Rainbow Reef, as well as other world-class dive sites. If you haven't qualified as a scuba-diver before you leave on your trip, this is a perfect opportunity to learn in crystal clear waters and warm temperatures.

Then there are the island resorts that are ideal for honeymooners and the incurable romantics. Islands such as Matamanoa and Tokoriki are great places to relax and self indulge. For something truly special for couples in search of something more, exclusive award winning resorts like Likuliku, are destinations in themselves.

Below from top. Navutu Stars. Bedroom at Navutu Star. Bath by candlelight at Navutu Star.

Stylish Places to Stay & Eat

Fijian fun: Vatulele. Vatulele is one of the largest islands with deluxe beach villas set in a natural jungle. There's a five-star PADI dive centre, where you can learn to dive and explore the incredible marine life and shipwrecks. There is a 5-mile long white beach perfect for evening walks and traditional Fijian BBQs which are held once a week.

Lovers paradise: Likuliku Lagoon Resort. Located in the Mamanuca group, featuring Fiji's only over-water bungalows, decorated like a typical Fijian village with traditional architecture. If you want to push the boat out you can arrive in style by helicopter and be serenaded on arrival by all the staff. Bear in mind that this is a couple's only resort, so no children allowed.

Honeymoon heaven: Navutu Stars Resort. Nestled along 3 secluded bays on the island of Yaqeta in the Yasawas. This island resort offers 9 individually designed, thatched-roof beachfront bures, and two honeymoon suites featuring a private spa which are stretched along a white sandy beach. The delightful restaurant menu offers a fusion of Italian and Fijian cuisine and a great selection of wines from the old and new world vineyards. They also offer diving courses and yoga classes daily.

Opposite page. Canoeists in Bora Bora.

Adventure: Culture + Art
Destination: French Polynesia

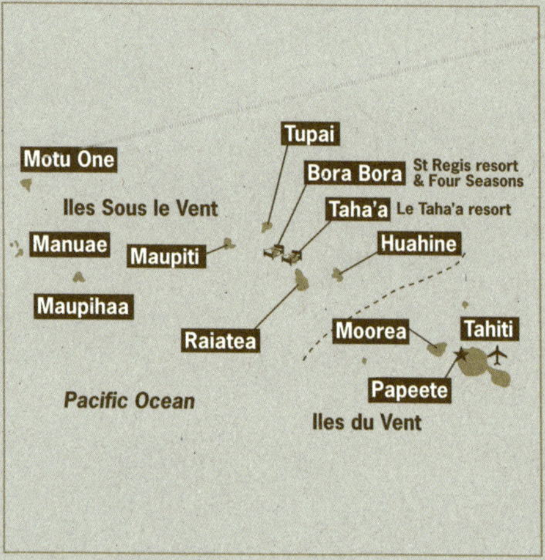

Regional Information

If there is a 'major league' of dramatically beautiful islands, then French Polynesia is top of the pile, it is also deeply rich in traditions, culture (inherited from their Maohi ancestors) and the historical sights make it pretty unique. This is especially true of the notoriously idyllic (but expensive) Society Islands. French Polynesia refers to five archipelagoes spread over an expanse of the South Pacific approximately the size of Western Europe (5,000,000 square kilometres). The region includes the Society Islands (with Tahiti, Moorea and Bora Bora as the best known islands), the Australs, the Marquesas, the Tuamotus and the Gambiers.

The Society Islands, (which still belong to France) are a collection of 15 large volcanic islands which are considered 'Paradise on Earth' by savvy travellers and were explored by Captain Cook and William Bligh, but they were made truly famous by the paintings of the artist, Paul Gauguin, and by the words of author, James A. Michener. Like the vast majority of visitors to the region, Gauguin was inspired by French Polynesia's turquoise lagoons, multi-coloured reef fish, volcanic peaks, lush valleys and white-sand beaches. Divided into two groups are the Windward Islands (Iles du Vent), and the Leeward Islands (Iles Sous le Vent) they were given their stylish names by Captain Cook in 1769, after England's Royal Society.

Most of these rugged islands are volcanic in origin, with a few small coral atolls mixed in. Of these, the most recognizable names are the legendary islands of Bora Bora, Huahine, Moorea and Tahiti.

Tahiti which has the best scope for exploring the fantastic tropical scenery and mountain ranges is the largest of the French Polynesian islands and was the first to be discovered by European explorers in the late 18th century. A great majority of the territory's population lives on Tahiti, especially in and around Papeete, the capital.

Today this busy little city has so many cars, trucks, and motor scooters that it can take up to 2 hours to commute to from the outlying regions. Although Papeete has lost much of its old South Seas charm, Tahiti's rural areas still display aspects of traditional Polynesia. Tropical flowers are everywhere on the islands, particularly in the hair of Tahitians. The Tiare Tahiti flower is used for greeting visitors on arrival and returning family. Tradition holds that, if taken, women and men wear a flower behind their left ear. Moorea is a charming island, clearly visible from Tahiti and just a 15-minute flight or hour ferry ride. Moorea is much more laid back than Tahiti, has some nice beaches along its north and west coasts and the spectacular settings of Cook's Bay and Opunohu Bay.

One of the world's most romantic honeymoon destinations, Bora Bora is famous for its world-class lagoon, and top-end luxury resorts. Out of which rises the main island topped by the dramatic, tombstonelike Mount Otemanu. Whilst exclusive resorts dominate these islands, if you can afford it, it is worth splurging out for a couple of days before moving on to the more rugged and less visited islands of Huahine, Raiatea or Taha'a.

Raiatea & Taha'a offer exceptional sailing and are a good choice for those who want to experience the Tahiti of old, with a few gem islands to visit in the lagoon on a day tour. Raiatea is only slightly smaller than Tahiti itself, and is recognized throughout Tahiti as it's 'Sacred Island' - the cultural heart of all Tahiti Polynesia. It is believed by historians that Raiatea was the main stopover point for early Polynesians who arrived from Hawaii, then known as Hav'aii.

Huahine is perhaps the most scenic, with gorgeous beaches and lagoon islands and is thought by the locals as 'Old Polynesia'. The locals call it 'wild' because of its undeveloped status. Here you can explore some of the region's most important archaeological sites. Huahine has many ancient maraes (traditional Polynesian temples).

Adventure: Culture + Art
Destination: French Polynesia

The open-air sanctuaries called marae were once the centre of power in ancient Polynesia. These stone religious sites, akin to temples, hosted the important events of the times such as the worship of the gods, peace treaties, celebrations of war, and the launch of voyages to colonize distant lands. One of the best persevered sites in the Maeva marae, (a former royal village) located at the foot of Mount Mouatapu and on the shores of Lake Fauna Nui.

Off to the northeast, the line of atolls known as the Tuamotu Archipelago boasts French Polynesia's top scuba diving destinations. Rangiroa, which encloses the world's second largest lagoon, is known for its clear waters, which are home to thousands of sharks. Sitting next to Rangiroa, Tikehau is considerably smaller, and its one international-standard resort sits on an islet all to itself. Also much smaller and shallower than the lagoon at Rangiroa, the fish-filled lagoon at Manihi makes it the world's largest producer of black pearls (a good local purchase if you can afford them) Further afield are the wildly beautiful Marquesas Islands, recently made famous by the TV's 'Survivor' show. The original settlers from the Western Polynesian islands brought with them a cultural legacy which remained woven through the fabric of Marquesan society. As certain myths, legends and beliefs were carried throughout the Polynesian world, so were distinctive images, implements and aesthetic ideals. Of these, the image most favoured by Marquesan artisans was that of the wise and potent ancestor Tiki, recognized generally through Polynesia as the creator of the human race. Tiki is frequently found in carved large freestanding wood and stone figures and on bowls, dishes, canoe paddles, and many objects of personal adornment, such as tattoos.

The word 'tatau' originated in Tahiti. The legend of Tohu, the god of tattoo, describes painting all the oceans' fish in colors and patterns. In Polynesian culture, tattoos have long been considered signs of beauty, and in earlier times were an important part of the culture in signaling adolescence. There are several places you can observe a tattooist at work, and if you desire to mark you body then these artists can design something unique for you.

The beauty of today's Tahitian dance testifies to its resilience in Polynesian culture. In ancient times, dances were linked with all aspects of life. One would dance to welcome a visitor, pray, challenge an enemy, and seduce a mate. Today's dance is still accompanied by traditional instruments such as thunderous drums and conch shells. Modern Tahitian music is popular worldwide with a sound that blends Polynesian rhythm and Western melody.

Heiva i Tahiti is the greatest Polynesian cultural event in the world. This celebration of ancient traditions and competitions has been the most important event in Tahiti for over 125 years. Visitors are encouraged to join in the celebration from late June to late July every year and discover daily and nightly events and displays. Tahitians gather in Papeete from many islands to display their crafts and compete in traditional sporting and musical events. A fabulous time to visit if you get the opportunity.

Below from top. Bungalows at St Regis.
Interior of overwater bungalow at Le Taha'a.
Le Taha'a.

Stylish Places to Stay & Eat

Super luxe: St Regis. Noted as a favourite amongst Hollywood stars as its secluded, extravagant and ludicrously expensive - but worth the splurge if you can afford it. You'll have a private butler attending to your every whim, and whilst most of the bungalows are positioned overwater, the best ones by far are the private suites with their own plunge pools. The restaurants are varied from a Japanese sushi bar to a seafood restaurant perched overlooking the sea.

Stylish retreat: Le Taha'a. For huge over-water villas, fabulous French-Polynesian food and some of the best coral and snorkelling in the region. Away from the resorts, there aren't many eating out but try 'Quai des Pecheurs' for fish and sashimi.

Adventure & action: Keikahanui Nuku Hiva Pearl Lodge. Located in a magnificent tropical garden, the lodge overlooks the bay and village of Taiohae, in the Marquesas Islands. The black sandy beach lying 50 steps below is an unusual setting. Take a jeep safari to discover archaeological sites steeped in ancient culture, enjoy a horseback or bicycle ride. If you are wanting hiking adventures this place is perfect.

Opposite page. Exterior of Pacific Resort Suite, Aitutaki .

Adventure: Spa
Destination: Cook Islands

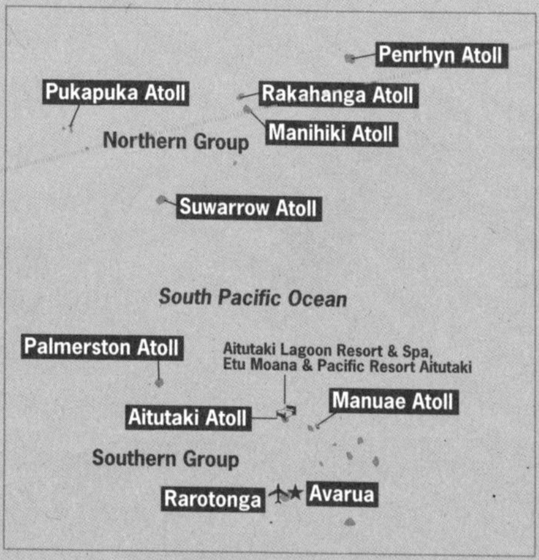

Regional Information

Only 800km (500 miles) west of Tahiti (virtually next door in this part of the world), the tiny Cook Islands have much in common with French Polynesia, both in physical beauty and people. Dreamy white sand beaches and sunny tropical islands with sheltered, clear blue turquoise lagoons and luxurious spa treatments for every ailment. Comprising of 15 islands, this carefree culture of song, dance and age old traditions is so much a part of the Cook Islands way of life.

The Cook Islanders share with the Tahitians a fun-loving lifestyle, many old Polynesian legends and gods, and about 60% of their native language. The Cooks were governed by New Zealand from 1901 until 1965 and still are associated with New Zealand. Consequently, Cook Islanders speak English fluently, which makes it easy for English-speaking travellers to take advantage of the South Pacific's most informative cultural tours and exhibits. They also pay less for almost everything and use the New Zealand dollar as their local currency, which means the Cooks are more affordable than French Polynesia for honeymooners watching their pocket.

Barely 32km (20 miles) around, Rarotonga is a miniature Tahiti in terms of its mountains, beaches, and reefs - but in terms of development, it's like Tahiti was some 50 years ago. Unlike Papeete, however, the capital of the Cook Islands, Avarua, remains a quiet little backwater, a picturesque village without a stoplight. Yet no other South Pacific destination has as many hotels, restaurants, daytime activities, and nightclubs packed into so small a space as does Rarotonga.

Opposite page from top. Room in the Pacific Resort, Aitutaki. Kayaking at the Pacific Resort, Aitutaki. Beach at the Pacific Resort, Aitutaki.

Adventure: Spa
Destination: Cook Islands

Among the outer islands, Aitutaki bears the same relationship to Rarotonga as Bora Bora does to Tahiti (but less expensive). Heavenly Aitutaki is known as a haven for romance with days spent relaxing, swimming and snorkelling in the lagoon with enough space and solitude to have that precious time together. Even if you don't stay in Aitutaki its worth a side trip just to explore the lagoons and the little islands fringing the reef. There are excursions to Aitutaki and you can fly with Air Rarotonga to Aitutaki and enjoy the 'Circle Island Tour' before boarding the 71 foot traditionally designed catamaran Titi Ai Tonga. Spend five hours cruising around the lagoon, enjoying lunch, allowing plenty of time to swim and snorkel in the crystal clear waters before heading back to Rarotonga. These trips can be booked independently with local companies.

Take a day cruise on the lagoon with snorkelling, visiting uninhabited motus (islets) and a beach barbeque – where you can eat at a table in the water to keep cool with a local company Teking Cruises. Teking also organise 'champagne breakfasts' on Maina Island which is a lovely treat for some seclusion and privacy. If you can keep up with the locals, go dancing at Spiders nightclub and for a change of pace and have dinner at Pacific Resort's great open-air restaurant.

Polynesian massages are very popular across the entire South Pacific. Samoans, Tahitians, Cook Islanders, Tongans, and the Niuean and Maoris all have their own speciality treatments. Experiencing a traditional massage in the Cook Islands is perhaps one of the most incredible relaxing and rejuvenating experiences, especially for a couple who experience a treatment together in a double room.

Polynesian Massage is generally regarded form of healing. Traditional therapy that is still practiced since the first arrival of Europeans to the homelands. Handed down through the generations this massage is passed down within villages or families. There are only a handful of healers still teaching and utilising the gift of healing from long ago.

Long flowing strokes along the body performed on the table or a traditional island mat. Traditional oils are used to help with the manipulation of the muscular, skeletal, nervous, lymph and circulatory systems of the body. The movements are performed not only by the hands and fingers but also by the elbow and forearms, to help regulate the body and relieve muscular aches and pains without causing discomfort. It is the combining of Swedish, Asian & Polynesian techniques to provide relaxation & remedial massage. It has different variations from island to island but the techniques used are the same. The only difference is the prayers coming from the practitioner or the person providing the bodywork. Ideal for those who need instant relief from pain, emotional release from Stress or who would like to try something different that leaves you feeling light as a feather and rejuvenated. Many of the main resorts offer a variety of treatments from massages to beauty treatments and facials. You can also look for independent Polynesian practitioners in the Cook Islands, if you prefer to use someone more specialised.

Stylish Places to Stay & Eat

Secluded luxury: Pacific Resort Aitutaki. This charming retreat shares top billing in the Cook Islands with the Aitutaki Lagoon Resort & Spa. Separated by foliage, 18 spacious bungalows stand on a flat shelf of land beside the beach. All of these have lagoon-facing porches and substantial baths with glass-enclosed showers. Local islanders make music after dark, and troupes perform their famous Cook Islands dances one night a week. The spa offers special signature 'skin' treatments for men, and Aitutaki exfoliation scrubs.

Spa in style: Aitutaki Lagoon Resort & Spa. The only resort on the islands located on its own private spot, and features 37 Bungalows, some of which are overwater The restaurant is perfect for moonlight romantic dinners and by day the activities include sea kayaking, mountain biking or enjoying a world-class spa experience at the Polynesian spa. Signature treatments include a 'Mirimiri' aromatherapy massage, where you can choose between different oils to aid relaxation or relieve tension.

Small & chic: Etu Moana. Pretty and private villas set in a lush garden setting overlooking the lagoon. This is self-catering so you'll have to make your own arrangements for dinner, top of the list should be 'Tapunas' restaurant. Make sure you take the fabulous captain Puna's 'yellow boat lagoon' cruise, which is voted as guest's most favourite excursion.

Opposite page. Santo Woman in Vanuatu courtesy of C Eric Lafforgue.

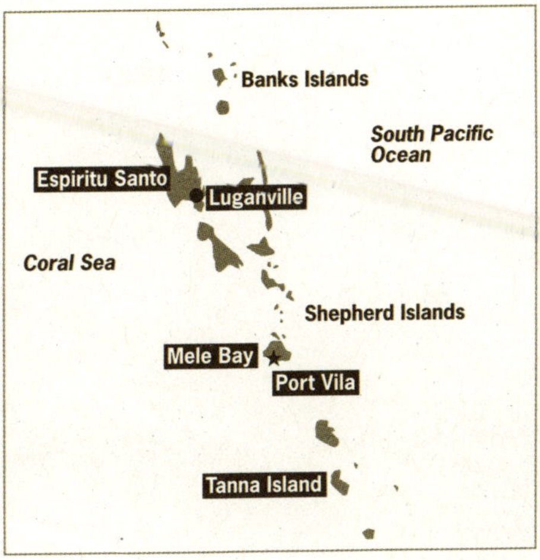

Focus On...
Shipwrecked on Vanuatu

In only three hours you can be in Vanuatu, the heart of Melanesia an archipelago of 83 islands. Vanuatu is a Y-shaped chain of 83 islands lying 2500km northeast of Sydney (Australia), 2000km north of Auckland (New Zealand), and 800km west of Nadi (Fiji). It is steeped in tradition and culture offering an abundance of stunning natural beauty and unique experiences... coral reefs, culinary delights, active volcanoes, shipwrecks and land diving just to name a few.

Port Vila is the hub of Vanuatu and is a great area for watersports, cruising, shopping and eating out. If you're interested in diving, Espiritu Santo (meaning holy spirit), the largest island in Vanuatu is a must. For a traditional experience take a trip to Tanna Island with its active volcano.

You think Vanuatu's beaches are unbeatable on one island until you reach the next, there are 83 islands to choose from so it's likely you'll have complete seclusion. Divers are delighted at the clear waters, coral reefs and shipwrecks; vulcanologists go wild for its many smoking peaks; and naturalists lust after its untouched forests, reefs and extravagant bird life.

The people of Vanuatu, a name that means 'Land Eternal', are predominantly Melanesian. The Ni Vanuatu have populated these islands for centuries and with more than 115 distinctly different cultures and languages still thriving here, Vanuatu is recognized as one of the most culturally diverse countries in the world. A few days exploring this less-touristic region can really enhance your experience of South Pacific.

Stylish Essentials

General Information

South Pacific Tourism Organisation
P.O Box 13119
Suva Fiji Islands
www.spto.org
T. +679 (0) 330 4177

Diving Adventures
PADI Worldwide Diving Information
www.padi.com

Airlines

The Great Escapade (RTW Airpass)
Air New Zealand, Singapore & Virgin Atlantic
www.thegreatescapade.com
T. 0800 028 4149
(UK Air New Zealand reservations)
T. 0870 190 4466
(UK Virgin Atlantic reservations)

Star Alliance (RTW Airpass)
Air New Zealand & Singapore Airlines.
www.staralliance.com

Air Fiji Ltd
www.airfiji.com
T.+ 679 (0) 3477 160

Air Tahiti Nui
www.airtahitinui.com
T. +689 (0) 460 303

Air Vanuatu
www.airvanuatu.com
T. +678 (0) 23 878

Air New Zealand
www.airnewzealand.co.nz
www.airnewzealand.com
T. 0800 028 4149 (UK reservations)

Air Rarotonga Ltd
www.airraro.com
T. +682 (0) 22890

British Airways
www.ba.com
T. 0844 493 0787
(UK reservations & enquiries)

Turtle Airways (sea plane in Fiji)
www.turtleairways.com
T. +679 (0) 6721 888

Private Yacht Charters
South Pacific & Australia
www.paradiseadventures.com.au

Fiji Seaplanes
www.fijiseaplanes.com

Fiji

Awesome Adventures
Denarau Marina, Nadi, Fiji
www.awesomefiji.com
T. +679 (0) 675 0499
E. info@awesomefiji.com

Yacht charters & sailing trips
P.O.Box 10562, Nadi Airport
www.sailingfiji.com
T. +679 (0) 672 5525

Fijian Kava Information
www.fijian-kava.com

Shark Diving
Beqa Adventure Divers
www.fiji-sharks.com

Navutu Stars Resort
P.O. Box 1838
Lautoka
www.navutustarsfiji.com
T. +679 (0) 664 0553
E. reservations@navutustarsfiji.com

Likuliku Lagoon Resort
PO Box 10044, Malolo Island, Mamanucas, Fiji
www.likulikulagoon.com
T. +679 (0) 666 3344
E. enquiries@likulikulagoon.com

Vatulele
Vatulele Island, Fiji
www.vatulele.com
T. +679 (0) 672 0300
E. Reservations-vatulele@sixsenses.com

French Polynesia

General Information
www.huahine.com

Tahiti Heiva Festival
contact@tahiti-heiva.org
www.tahiti-heiva.org

Moorea Tattoo
Specialist in Tattoo Art
PK 32 Cote Montagne
Haapiti-varari
Moorea
www.mooreatattoo.com
T. +689 (0) 76 4260

St Regis
Motu Ome'e BP 506
Bora Bora 98730
www.starwoodhotels.com/stregis
T. +689 (0) 60 78 88

Le Taha'a
www.letahaa.com
T. +689 (0) 60 84 00
E. infos@letahaa.com
F. +689 (0) 60 84 01

Keikahanui Nuku Hiva Pearl Lodge
Nuku Hiva Taiohae
Marquesas Islands,
French Polynesia
www.pearlresorts.com/keikahanui

Cook Islands

General Information
www.aitutakitourism.com

Teking Lagoon Cruises
P.O BOX 117 Aitutaki Aitutaki,
Cook Islands
T. +682 (0) 31582

Aitutaki Lagoon Resort & Spa
Motu Akitua
Aitutaki Lagoon
Cook Islands
www.aitutakilagoonresort.com
T. +682 (0) 31203

Etu Moana
Etu Moana
P.O. Box 123
Aitutaki
Cook Islands
www.etumoana.com
T. +682 (0) 31458

Pacific Resort Aitutaki
P.O Box 90
Amuri
Aitutaki Cook Islands
www.aitutaki.pacificresort.com
T. +682 (0) 31720

Cristo Redentor, Rio de Janeiro.

BRAZIL

Rio de Janeiro | Salvador da Bahia |
Iguaçu falls | The Amazon |

BRAZIL

Why is this place so special?

Images of Brazil, for most, seem to conjure up impressions of carnivals, football and good looking scantily glad girls (and boys) playing volleyball on a beach. Brazil might easily be the most exhibitionist and vibrant country on the planet, famed for their unbridled pursuit of pleasure and happiness. It's one of those destinations that is on many travellers tick list, whether it's the rainforests, steakhouses, parties or beaches; Brazil really is infectious.

Brazil is also the largest country in South America and thus has a wide range of weather patterns making its biodiversity large and extreme, from mountains to rainforests, beaches to giant waterfalls. Its position in South America makes it easy to reach and can be coupled together with visiting one of the many 10 neighbouring South American countries. Brazil's rainforests and plethora of activities make it an excellent choice for honeymooners wanting to escape the normal honeymoon scene, and for those who like to keep busy; from rafting, trekking, horse-riding, mountain biking or cultural activities such as samba dancing to music classes or watching a raucous sporting event. Gastronomy is also extremely varied due to the influence derived from being colonized by Portugal, during the African slave trade and influence from Asian immigrants. The classic Brazilian dish 'Feijoada' which is a kind of stew of black beans and meat is not to be missed.

From top. Ipanema Beach. Cristo Redentor. View out over ocean from Zank Boutique Hotel, Salvador de Bahia.

The most visited places in Brazil include Rio de Janeiro (there is nothing in the world quite like Carnival in Rio) and Sao Paulo (the two bustling megacities of the south-east), the more relaxed city of Salvador in the northeast, or the old colonial towns of Ouro Preto and Olinda. For natural beauty, visiting Iguaçu Falls and spending a few days hiking around the area is a must. A couple of weeks in Brazil, starting with exploring the glamorous city of Rio for a few days, trekking the Amazon for a week, then a few days on the coast or perched overlooking Iguaçu fall should be ample time; better still if you have a month you certainly won't be short of things to see and do. The variety of accommodation in Brazil is vast from boutique gems to hip retreats and eco-lodges dotting the country, so there is something for every budget.

Fast Facts

Capital: Brasilia.

Location: Brazil has ten neighbours: the Department of French Guiana and the countries of Suriname, Guyana, Venezuela and Colombia to the north; Uruguay and Argentina to the south; and Paraguay, Bolivia and Peru to the west.

Population: 186,112,794.

Religion: Roman Catholic 73.6%, Protestant 15.4%, Spiritualist 1.3%, Bantu/voodoo 0.3%, other 9.4%.

Languages: Portuguese is the official language of Brazil. Except for the languages spoken by Indian tribes living in remote reservations, Portuguese is the only language of daily life.

Opposite page from top. Maracana soccer stadium. Meeting of the waters in the Amazon courtesy of Dreamstime. Iguaçu falls.

Getting there and exploring around

Most travellers fly into São Paulo or Rio de Janeiro as these are the countries main international gateways. Although it is possible to arrive overland especially from Argentina (many visitors at Iguaçu falls stay on both sides of the border), Peru and Bolivia. You can buy South American air passes (LAN or TAM) which are valid for 21 days, so if you are visiting other countries this might be more convenient and economical.

Getting around Brazil can be a challenge because of the sheer vastness of the country. Although there are plenty of highways and buses, often air travel is preferred, especially if you are short of time. Thanks to a recent increase in competition from domestic no-frills carrier Gol, the regular fares on the main domestic carriers have come down quite a bit. For those travelling larger distances in Brazil there is also the option of purchasing an air pass (much to the envy of Brazilians this pass is available to foreigners only). Often these Air passes need to be purchased and booked outside of Brazil.

If you have longer bus travel can be comfortable and affordable. Tickets can be purchased ahead of time with reserved seats. All buses are non-smoking, and in most cases people adhere to the regulations. On many popular routes travellers can opt for a deluxe coach with air-conditioning and leito (seats that recline almost flat).

Car rentals are expensive, and the distances are huge, as an example Salvador to Rio is a 1,800km (1,116-mile) drive. Within Brazilian cities, renting a car is only for the bold: drivers are aggressive, rules sporadically applied, and parking a competitive sport – you may also find yourself being 'spot-checked' by police looking for illegal substances, which can be a bit nerve-racking especially if you don't speak basic Portuguese.

Best time of year to visit

Although most of Brazil lies in the tropics, more than 60 percent of the population live in areas which are cooled either by altitude, sea winds or polar fronts. While the coastal cities of Rio de Janeiro, Recife and Salvador can get extremely hot, plateau cities such as São Paulo, Brasília and Belo Horizonte have much milder climates, and the Southern cities of Porto Alegre and Curitiba have a climate similar to that of Southern Europe. Travelling in and around Brazil can be busy during the following annual events:

- New Year: December 31 - January 1 - known locally as Ano Nove. Accommodation in Rio de Janeiro can be especially difficult to find during this period as up to 2 million people gather to party the night away.
- Carnival Rio: late February - early March - when finding accommodation anywhere in Brazil can be difficult.
- Independence Day: September 7 - fortunately, unlike carnival, this is only a one-day event as the whole country comes to a standstill!

If you are intending on visiting Brazil's pristine beaches; keep in mind that the beaches are on the Atlantic coast, so you should try to avoid travelling during June to August, when the sea can be notoriously rough and cold.

? Must know before you go

Learn the lingo. Brazil is the largest and most populated of all the South American countries. But don't attempt to speak Spanish if travelling in Brazil - this can be quite insulting as they are a Portuguese-speaking nation with a decidedly different colonial past to their neighbours!

Conversing. Brazilians tend to be very zesty and passionate individuals. To foreigners, their conversations may seem vivacious and quick, characterised by much interjection and interruption. So don't take the interruptions as rude and overbearing; it is actually a mark of enthusiasm an interest in what you are saying.

Samba! Brazilians love to dance in a fiery, passionate and sensual way. Close personal space, with a degree of touching of the arms, back and hands whilst in conversation are not uncommon. As a foreigner you should be prepared for this close proximity in personal space. It would be bad etiquette to shuffle away or seem offended by the close contact.

Highlights

Head for heights. For a treat, hire a helicopter to pluck you out of Rio early afternoon and stop off on a jetty by a fabulous seafood restaurant on Ilha Grande.

Great gastronomy. Explore the historic centre, immerse yourselves in the culture of Salvador and feast on fusion Bahian cuisine.

Cascading crusade. Take a shower at Iguaçu falls. Take a boat to 'devils throat' the most majestic of Iguaçu's cascades.

Nature trek. Trek the Amazon jungle, experience the vast wildlife and nature at its best.

Tip for the Trip

"'If you are intending an extended visit in a country or region check before you leave if there are special air passes available to foreigners. In Brazil and Japan for example there are special rates, but only for foreigners. These also must be purchased before leaving your country of residence."

Jill

Opposite page. Top. Rio Carnival.
Bottom. Leblon by night.

Adventure: City
Destination: Rio de Janeiro

Regional Information

Rio de Janeiro a marvellous city, dramatically set between rainforest clad cliffs and the sea is always awash with joyful existence. Locals love Rio calling it 'cidade maravilhosa' and referring to themselves as 'Cariocas' for being part of what is undoubtedly the world's most beautiful city setting (with the worlds most beautiful people). Rio may be famed for its 4-day annual carnival, (usually in February/March) but there is much more to this city than just festivals and parties.

It is also one of the most famous and visited, with its Christ Redeemer as the main attraction and two of the world's most famous beaches, Ipanema and Copacabana, (and lessen known Leblon and Flamengo) anchoring Rio's 45 miles of white sand beaches. Whilst many tourists are initially attracted to luxurious Copacabana Palace, it isn't situated in the most desirable spot in town. Copacabana beach is a little run-down and is very touristy. If you are insistent on visiting here, then drink a Cipriani on the terrace at the Copacabana Palace should satisfy the curiosity.

Away from the beaches you will find much art by contemporary artists in galleries and museums, excellent shopping particularly for jewellery, plentiful hotels in all price ranges and a huge variety of restaurants. The breathtaking views at the top of the 396 metre of Sugarloaf Mountain (Pão de Acúcar), as well as the Tijuca rainforest (only 15 minutes away); yet adventurous visitors can find plentiful urban cultural adventures in this special city with 7 million native hosts.

One of the most thrilling sites in Rio is Corcovado, a mountain with a sheer granite face topped by the Cristo Redentor (Christ the Redeemer) statue rising more than 100 feet from a 20-foot pedestal. You can reach the top on an 1885 cogwheel train or on a winding road with great beach views. A lovely way to get a birds eye view is to take a helicopter trip around the statue, and watching the sunset or sunrise cán be extremely romantic.

MANGUEIRA
EMBARQUE
DESEMBARQUE

Adventure: City
Destination: Rio de Janeiro

The second famous peak, Sugarloaf Mountain, is just as impressive, giving a different perspective of the city. Sugarloaf consists of a huge granite slab at the entrance of the Guanabara Bay. From the top at 1,295 feet, (photo 50-4), you can see the whole city, plus the beaches and the Atlantic Ocean. To ascend, you catch a two-stage cableway with a length of 4,265 feet. The sunsets as seen from the top are equally fabulous.

Few sporting events can rival a Brazilian football match. Brazil has won the FIFA World Cup tournament a record five times, in 1958, 1962, 1970, 1994 and 2002 and is the only team to have never missed a World Cup participation, and to be among the favorites to win the trophy every time the competition is scheduled. Pelé, one of the most recognized footballers in history, led Brazil to three of those championships and is the top scorer of all time in the sport. There is no doubt that football in Brazil is an institution and more so a religion for men, women and children. The Brazilian football year is split into 2 seasons late July to early December and late January to early June. Tickets are normally available from the ground on a match day, although some of the big clashes you may need to book ahead. The Maracana soccer stadium is one of the biggest football stadiums in the world, and is worth visiting even if there is no match playing.

Another Brazilian passion is dancing and music. The original samba schools originated in Rio de Janeiro in 1928. In 1930, thanks to President Getulio Vargas, the samba schools became an official part of Rio's world-famous carnival. However, it took years for the notion to gain national esteem. The original three schools were Estação de Sá, Estação Primeira de Mangeira, and Portela. Today, 14 principal samba schools spend the entire year, as well as lavish amounts of money, preparing what they hope to be the best performance to date. Usually the family tradition is to hand down samba from generation to generation with the main goal of performing spectacular carnival parades during carnival each year (occurring during the lent season).

Often, samba schools have impact on whole 'bairros' or city parts, with thousands of Cariocas (people born and raised in Rio) adjoining the rehearsals with dancing, singing and samba!

Tourists visiting Rio should stop by one of the schools for some samba dancing instruction, as the schools are open to the public from December to March. If you want to experience Brazil, you have to learn some samba dance moves; equally it's a good way to learn a skill with your new spouse. You can also experience the thrill of performing in the world's most exciting carnival as an insider. Many samba schools do offer you the opportunity to join them in their stunning costumes, mesmerizing dance routines, and over-the-top excitement.

Below from left. Bedroom at La Suite. Breakfast at La Suite.

Stylish Places to Stay

Elegant & fabulous: Fasano. Designed by Philippe Starck with Art Deco lamps, marble bathrooms and quirky fittings; the beds have 300 thread-count Egyptian linens and plump goose-down pillows – perfect for an early night. The rooftop infinity pool has incredible views and guest are given complimentary Havaianas (flip flops).

Exclusive retreat: La Suite. An indulgent, intimate and quiet guesthouse, with only 7 themed rooms, is the owner's former private home. It's a secluded location (just outside central Rio) with tremendous views and it's within walking distance from Joatinga beach. The best room is the 'black suite' with 2 marble bathrooms and windows facing the sea.

Budget boutique: Mama Ruisa. Fabulous 19th-century guesthouse with views over the Guanabara bay, some rooms have terraces and the pool is divine. They also offer a very personal service; they can arrange massages, private tours and tips of what to do, where to eat and where to avoid!

Delicious Places to Eat

Served in style: Zuka. Bright and modern and one of the trendiest restaurants in Rio. The simple, wooden tables surround a sunken kitchen, where diners can watch their meals being prepared. The food is delicious, but it is the presentation that lingers in the memory. Served on big rectangular plates, each dish is a work of art. The three course lunch deal for £13 is a bargain.

Sweet and chic: La Suite. Simply the best modern French cuisine in Rio, with a Brazilian twist, using only the finest local ingredients and served on a stunning terrace.

Meat madness: Espírito Santa. One of Santa Teresa's best new restaurants serves delectable meat and seafood dishes from the Amazon, which you can enjoy on the back terrace, with its sweeping views. On the ground floor is the main dining room and bar and a spacious veranda with a view of the historic neighbourhood.

Oppostie page. Clockwise from top. Capoeira in Salvador. Salvador de Bahia, courtesy of Dreamstime. Vista acrea Praia do Forte.

Adventure: Gastronomy **Destination:** Salvador da Bahia

Regional Information

Bahia is one of the largest States of Brazil; with 567,295 km2, it´s slightly smaller than France. The population of over 13 million concentrates mostly along the coast; Salvador, the capital, is the most important city and is located on the Bay of All Saints. Salvador is often termed 'the land of the drums' as it's Brazil's capital of African culture, which is shown in everything from the food to the music to capoeira (Brazilan martial arts). A week is perfect time to explore the area, enjoy some excellent cuisine and soak up the atmosphere.

The historical centre of Salvador is still essentially as it was in the 16th century, despite the city's expansion it has managed to preserve some magnificent examples of Renaissance architecture. Multicoloured homes, red-tiled roofs, a wonderful market, twisting and narrow cobblestone streets, great beaches and around 300 churches make a romantic and compelling place to visit. However, it is the world class eclectic gastronomy of this region that really stands out.

In 1533, the Portuguese colonized Brazil and after a lengthy Moorish occupation, Portugal had adapted a variety of North African cooking traditions, among them coffee, dried fruits and pastries. These culinary customs were in turn exported to Brazil, with the twist of being prepared using local ingredients. The largest single influence on Brazilian cuisine came with African slaves. Dende, peppers and coconut milk, staples of West African cooking, became firmly established on the Brazilian palate, which is partly why today you can taste African fusion cooking everywhere.

Adventure: Gastronomy
Destination: Salvador da Bahia

Salvador has its own exotic cuisine, influenced by three main ingredients: coconut milk; the spicy malagueta pepper; and dendê oil - all present in the delicious moqueca (seafood stew). Bobó is similar to moqueca but is thickened with the addition of mashed aipim (manioc). The flavour base of these two dishes is similar to the ingredients in acarajés, including the ubiquitous dendé and coconut milk. Bobós, moquecas, and most other traditional Bahian dishes are generally prepared and served in a bubbling panela de barro (clay pot). There are several cookery schools in the area, where you can learn the art of African/Brazilian fusion cuisine, the best one is SENAC which also has a restaurant.

There are essentially two neighbourhoods in Salvador Pelourinho (Pillory), and Barra (Bar, as in reef, and pronounced "BA-ha"), which has a number of hotels and the two beaches closest to the city centre (with the exception of some very small beaches frequented only by very local people). Barra also has the impressive Forte de Santo Antônio and Porto da Barra, which is a stunning white colonial fort at one end and a whitewashed church sitting up on a hill at the other. This makes a great place for evening walks watching the sun set.

Pelourinho, an old neighbourhood of Salvador, contains the most extensive example of baroque architecture in the Americas. Six hundred buildings in the area were immaculately restored and included by UNESCO (United Nations Educational, Scientific, and Cultural Organization) in its list of world heritage sites. The Pelourinho district is packed with restaurants, and there is a smattering of excellent eateries along the oceanfront.

Below from top. Zank Boutique Hotel.
Zank Boutique Hotel Restaurant.

Stylish Places to Stay

Gourmet Gastronomic: Kiaroa Eco-Luxury Resort. Set in an ecological sanctuary on the Marau peninsula, a short flight from Salvador serving exceptional gourmet gastronomy and a wonderful list of wine. The bungalows are all handcrafted using local materials and the wonderful spa has a list of treatments.

Zank Boutique Hotel. Located in trendy neighbourhood of Rio Vermelho and a few minutes away from Salvador centre, this small intimate boutique gem with only 20 rooms is divine. There are two themes to the grounds 'the old house' with baroque themes and the 'minimalist' section with classic contemporary style.

Cute Casa: Hotel Casa do Amarelindo. Nestled in a fully restored 19th century building in the heart of Pelhourinho, this hotel is conveniently located within easy reach of all the restaurants, bars, recreation facilities, festivals and shows which make this historical district of Salvador world-famous.

Delicious Places to Eat

Romantic charm: Dona Chika-Ka. Romantic candles lead the way up to a charmingly decorated dining room, where you can feast on local delicacies such as bobó de camarão and other Bahian food. Book a table outside on the cobblestone street and soak up the atmosphere.

Bahian in Barra: Pereira. If you are looking for a Bahia restaurant Salvador that specializes in Salvador food and drink then look no further than Pereira in the Barra neighbourhood. This restaurant serves beautiful South American dishes such as 'bolinho de bacalhau', or cod dumplings, its always busy so be sure to book.

Bahian fusion: Pelo Bistro. This restaurant/ bistro, situated in the hotel Casa do Amarelindo in Pelourinho has an outside dining room next to a walled garden, with an excellent wine list from Brazil & Argentina.

Opposite page. Iguaçu Falls, courtesy of Dreamstime.

Adventure: Action
Destination: Iguaçu falls

Regional Information

Iguassu Falls or Iguaçu Falls depending on which side of the border you are, literally means 'big water' which is something of an understatement. Situated on the border of Brazil, Argentina and Paraguay, the falls are surrounded by tropical forests and home to more than 2000 species of flora and 80 different mammals, with plenty of outdoor activities such as walking. This is a nature lover's and action hero's paradise.

Sometimes described as being one of the 7 natural Wonders of the World; in fact, Iguaçu Falls is neither the widest waterfall in the world, nor are they the tallest. However, what it lacks in width and height it makes up for elsewhere in terms of scenery. Iguazú is considered one of the four most spectacular waterfalls in the world, along with Niagara Falls (United States of America), Angel Falls (Venezuela) and Victoria Falls (Zambia and Zimbabwe).

On the Parana River, the falls act as a natural border to the countries of Brazil, Argentina and Paraguay and compose of 275 cataracts in total. The best time of year to see the Iguaçu Falls is between November and March (the rainy season) and as this is such a magnificent sight, it is highly recommended that you make arrangements to stay at least two or three nights to experience the area.

The most inspiring section of the falls is "The Devil's Throat", which is comprised of fourteen different falls that drop 350 feet to the rocks below, sending a plume of spray one hundred feet into the air. Between January to March it is the rainy season and the falls becomes even more impressive. There are five star hotels on both the Argentine and Brazilian sides near the falls. These are convenient, but there are cheaper options nearby.

Opposite page from left. Hotel Das Cataras. Brazilian steak.

Adventure: Action
Destination: Iguaçu falls

The falls area was formed ages ago when successive volcanic residue passed over the region. These volcanic layers eroded at different rates, and the falls were formed where the water flows from a slowly eroding layer. The falls are inching backwards as the water slowly erodes the upper layers of rock.

Once you've finished observing the falls (which may take a while), you can visit the parks themselves, which are home to a number of animal and bird species. Iguaçu National Park, on the Brazilian side, has 170,000 hectares of protected land. These parks have been a UNESCO World Heritage site since 1984 due to their beauty and biodiversity. There are many mammals, including five species of giant cat. There are also more than 450 species of birds in the area, including parrots, toucans and the rare great dusky swift. On both sides of the falls there are walking paths that lead you around and over the many small cascades that make up the falls. Exploring the paths on either side at a leisurely, pleasant pace will take several hours, but it's time well spent.

Other activities in the area include microflights or hang gliding lessons over the falls, which are a wonderful way to experience the falls from the sky. You can book day classes of a full course if you want to learn. There are also numerous boat companies that offer inflatable boat trips along the Iguaçu River, as well as 'rafting' experiences. These can be fun and a great way to explore the lush national park and forests. Some boats take 25 people, but be sure to ask for a 'private boat' if you want a more intimate experience.

Stylish Places to Stay

Traditional treat: Hotel Das Cataratas. The only hotel located actually inside the national park, although you can't see the falls from the hotel, it's only a 200m/656-ft. walk. Guests also have use of a large pool complex, and a forested area behind the hotel with nature walks and trails to explore. Their concierge offers walking, trekking and boat safari adventures for those who don't want to plan things independently. Opt for one of the suites in the main building with partial views of the falls.

Hillside luxury: Panoramic Hotel Iguazu. Located on the Argentinean side, this gives an entirely different perspective of the falls. It is located very close to the Three Frontiers Landmark, in the city of Puerto Iguazu and surrounded by lush tropical gardens. The most amazing aspect about this hotel for couples is the sunsets down by the pool.

Local & friendly: La Sorgente Hotel Posada. Excellent value for money, this family-run gem prides itself on a very personal friendly service. Breakfasts are well prepared and abundant, and the hotel's location, an easy walk from the restaurants and business district of Puerto Iguazu gives this hotel quite an advantage over many of the other lodgings that are out on the main highway.

Delicious Places to Eat

Piranha surprise: Clube Maringa. If you're in the mood for local fish, this is the place to come. The restaurant is located on the edge of the Rio Paraná, on the grounds of the local yacht club. For a prix fixe you can have the unlimited self-service buffet, plus a calderão (thick soup) of piranha and three fresh-fish dishes. Offerings change daily, but often include piapara fish grilled in a banana leaf, barbecued dourado, or surubi sautéed in butter.

Meat madness: Bufalo Branco Churrascaria. Likely the best place in the city for Brazilian churrasco (grilled meat). Appetizers from the grill include sausage, turkey breast with bacon, and chicken hearts at different cuisine levels from well done to rare (go for medium if you're not sure). They also offer popular cuts such as picanha (rump steak), alcatra (top sirloin), filet mignon, maminha (a fattier rump steak), and contra filet (entrecôte).

Spanish delights: Zaragoza. International cuisine with a strong Spanish flavour. On Saturday, there's a traditional Brazilian feijoada, and on Sunday they offer a paella for lunch. The wine list includes national and imported wines with the emphasis on Spanish, Argentine, and Portuguese.

Opposite page. Sailing in the Amazon river, courtesy of Dreamstime.

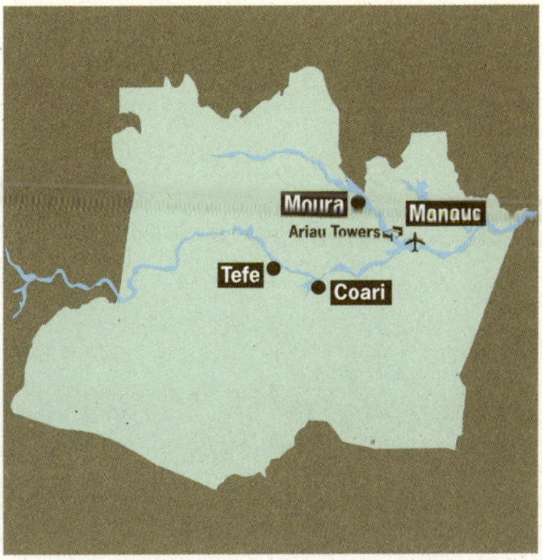

Focus On...
Action in the Amazonas

Amazonas is the largest state of Brazil, located in the northern part of the country. Neighbouring states are Roraima, Pará, Mato Grosso, Rondônia, Acre. It also borders Peru, Colombia and Venezuela. From the capital, Manaus, tours take tourists to see the meeting of waters where the rivers Negro and Solimões run alongside without mixing their waters, and stay in the lodges in the forest, appreciated by foreign tourists.

Covering an impressive 7 of Brazil's 27 states, "The Green Inferno" covers almost 40 per cent of Brazil's total landmass. Although parts of the Amazon cover countries bordering Brazil (notably Bolivia, Colombia, Guiana and Peru), it is to Brazil that most tourist come if they want to take in the splendours of this most magnificent natural wonder. Things to do in the Amazon include bird watching, trekking/hiking, climbing and taking boat journeys along the river. Without doubt, a tour to Brazil is incomplete without a trip to the Amazon.

Within 250km of Manaus are several luxury jungle lodges where you can get back to nature, such as Ariau Towers. Locally run Ariau Towers is designed to offer environmentalists an unforgettable experience, staying in eco friendly tree houses or Tarzan suites with 30ft high catwalks. Not for those who are adverse to heights! The hotel offers a range of adventure activities from fishing trips to tours of the Amazon – it's also been known to have attracted a range of well known celebrities from Susan Sarandon to Bill Gates.

ⓘ Stylish Essentials

Brazilian Embassy & Tourist Information
www.brazil.org.uk

Overview information for tourists
www.gringoes.com.br

Information of Rio
www.ipanema.com

Airlines

British Airways
www.ba.com
T. 0844 493 0 787
(UK reservations & enquiries)

Gol
www.voegol.com.br
T. +55 (0) 300 7892121
(Local number)

Varig
www.varig.com.br
T. +55 (0) 800 997 000
(Local number)

LAN Airlines
www.lan.com
T. 0800 977 6100
(UK reservations & enquiries)

TAM
www.tam.com.br
T. +55 (0) 800 123 100
Local number)

Rio de Janeiro

Samba Schools

Beija-Flor
Av. NSra. Copacabana, 1133 / conj. 201 - Copacabana
Rio de Janeiro - Rj - CEP 22070-011
www.beija-flor.com.br
T. +55 (0) 21 2247 4800

Mangueira
www.mangueira.com.br
T. +55 (0) 21 3872 6786
E. epm@mangueira.com.br

Portela
Rua Almirante Barroso, 5/6, Duque de Caxias

Império Serrano
Av. Ministro Edgard Romero,
114 Madureira, Rio de Janeiro
T. +55 (0) 21 3359 4944

Rio Carnival
www.rio-carnival.net
E. tickets@rio-carnival.net

Maracanã Soccer Stadium
www.suderj.rj.gov.br/maracana.asp
T. +55 (0) 21 2567 4945

Helicopter Flights
Helisights
www.helisight.com.br
T. +55(0) 21 2511 2141
(reservations)

Caipirinhas at Rio Scenarium
Rua do Lavradio, 20
Centro Antigo, Rio de Janeiro
www.rioscenarium.com.br
T. +55 (0) 21 3147 9005

Copacabana Palace, Avenida
Atlântica 1702, Copacabana
www.copacabanapalace.com.br
T. +55 (0) 21 2548 7070
E. reservas@copacabanapalace.com.br

Fasano
AV, Vieira Souto 80.
Rio de Janeiro
www.fasano.com.br
T. +55 (0) 21 3202 4000

Mama Ruisa
Rua Santa Cristina 132, Santa Teresa
Rio de Janeiro
www.mamaruisa.com
T. +55 (0) 21 2242 1281

La Suite
Rua Jackson de Figueiredo 501,
Joa, Rio de Janeiro
T. +55 (0) 21 2484 1962
E. lasuite.rio@gmail.com
(direct email for bookings)

Zuka
R dias Ferreira, 233b Leblon
Rio de Janeiro
www.zuka.com.br
T. +55 (0) 21 3205 7154

Espírito Santa
Rua Almirante Alexandrino 264
www.espiritosanta.com.br
T. +55 (0) 21 2508 7095
Open: Mon-Wed 11.30–18.00
Thu-Sat: 11.30–0.00
Sun: 11.30–19.00

Salvador da Bahia

Cookery schools
SENAC
Largo do Pelourinho 13-19,
Pelourinho
T. + 55 (0) 71 321 5502

Hotel Casa do Amarelindo
Rua das Portas do Carmo, N0.6
Pelourinho 40026-290 Salvador BA
www.casadoamarelindo.com
T. +55 71 3266 8550

Kiaroa Eco-Luxury Resort
Loteamento da Costa, área SD6,
Camamu, Barra Grande
Marau Peninsula, Bahia,
www.kiaroa.com.br
T. +55 (0) 71 3272 1320

Zank
Rua Almirante Barroso, 161
Rio Vermelho - Salvador
www.zankhotel.com.br
T. +55 (0) 71 3083 4000

Dona Chika-Ka
Rua João Castro Rabelo 10,
Pelourinho
T. +55 (0) 71 321 1712
Open: Dinner Mon-Sat

Pereira
Av 7 de Setembro
3959 Barra (nr Porto Seguro)
www.pereirarestaurante.com.br
T. +55 (0) 71 3264 6464
Open: Lunch Thurs-Sun, Dinner every night.

Pelo Bistro
Hotel Casa do Amarelindo, Rua das Portas do Carmo, 06,
Pelourinho, Salvador 40026-290,
T. +55 (0) 71 3266 8550

Iguaçu Falls

General Information
www.iguazuargentina.com

Microflights/ Hang Gliding
Weekend Fly
Sítio de Vuelo Iguaçu II –
Av. João Ricieri Maran - Três Lagoas
Foz do Iguaçu
www.weekendfly.com.br
T. +55 (0) 45 3577 5757

Helicopter rides
Helisul Táxi Aéreo Ltda.
Rodovia das Cataratas, Km 16,5 –
CEP 85863-000, Foz do Iguaçu
www.helisul.com
T. +55 (0) 45 3529 7474
E. atendimento@helisul.com

Boat trips & rafting at Iguaçu Falls - Macuco Safari
Cataratas Highway, km 25,
Iguaçu National Park, Iguaçu Falls
www.macucosafari.com.br
T. +55 (0) 45 523 6475 529

Panoramic Hotel Iguazu
Paraguay 372 N3370FKB
Puerto Iguazú, Misiones, Argentina
www.panoramic-hoteliguazu.com
T. +54 (0) 37 57498 133

Hotel Das Cataratas
Parque Nacional do Iguaçu
www.hoteldascataratas.com
T. + 55 (0) 45 2102 7000

La Sorgente Hotel Posada
Av Cordoba 454
Puerto Iguazu 3700 Argentina
www.lasorgenethotel.com
T. +54 (0) 3757 422 756

Bufalo Branco
Rua Engeneiro Reboucas 530,
Foz de Iguaçu
www.bufalobranco.com.br
T. +55 (0) 45 3523 9744

Clube Maringa
Rua Dourado 111, Foz de Iguaçu
T. +55 (0) 343527 9683

Zaragoza
Rua Quintini Bocaiuva 882,
Foz de Iguaçu
www.restaurantzaragoza.com.br
T. +55 (0) 453574 3084

Amazonas

Manaus Floating Tours
A three-hour tour visiting the highlights of Manaus from the Floating Docks to Teatro Amazonas
Rua José Paranaguá, 243
Manaus – Amazonas
www.orquideatours.com

Ariau Towers
www.ariautowers.com

Tips and advice

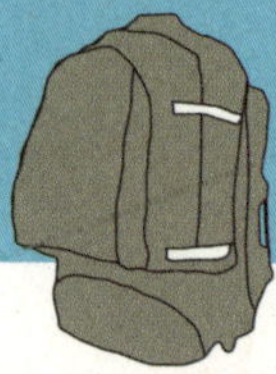

Stag & hen parties

It's becoming increasingly popular for groups to take breaks overseas, such as hiring a private villa in Spain, touring the vineyards in France, sailing in Croatia or ice-driving in Sweden. It can be a great way to bond with your friends before the big day, take some time out from work and get away from all the pressures. Delegate the party planning to your head hen or head stag, it'll be more fun and will leave you more time to take care of the big day.

Planning your honeymoon – a two part experience?

The most popular choice these days is a dual centred honeymoon, combining a week of beach-based relaxation with a more active or cultural-based week. This type of honeymoon can provide something for both of you, and also allow you the option to explore a couple of places rather than be 'stuck' in one spot. Before you start planning, think about what you both really enjoy and want from the honeymoon, if it's action, sight-seeing or cultural trips be honest, it is after all for both of you, not just a holiday for one.

Planning your honeymoon – when to start booking?

Some hotels and airlines don't release their prices more than a year in advance. If you are travelling during the 'peak season' as soon as prices are released, you need to start booking to secure your first choice. Start researching as early as possible so when prices are released you can book straight away. If you are booking independently then most hotels will require a credit card authorisation to secure a booking, but you can pay the balance on check-out. This does help with managing your cash flow, especially during the run-up to the big day when money will be running through your fingers!

Planning your honeymoon – the first night?

Chances are you're not jetting straight off on your honeymoon, so where do you spend your first night together as husband and wife? Decide whether you want to stay in the same hotel as some of your guests, or whether you would like to go somewhere completely different. Some couples like the idea of staying in the same place and being able to enjoy breakfast with their guests the next morning, while others want to be left alone. Whatever you decide to do, book it early as it's likely to be the most important night of your life.

Familymoons

Thinking of taking the kids with you on your honeymoon? More and more couples are having children before getting married, so it might be more practical if they accompany you on your honeymoon. Although make sure you plan some time out together as a couple, getting married is a big occasion and your children will want to be a part of it all. If you have very young children then opt for a destination closer to home, France and Italy are great destinations for 'familymoons.'

More honeymoon inspiration...

January

- Beach - head to a dreamy beach in the Philippines.
- Gastronomy - South Africa is perfect for food & wine lovers, in Cape Town or venture out on a safari in the Kruger national park.
- Action - try skiing in the Alpes, and a cosy lodge for two.

February

- Beach - dive, swim, snorkel and laze on the beautiful atolls of the Maldives.
- Culture - head to China for Chinese New Year. Hong Kong is one of Asia's most vibrant destinations.
- City - it's carnival time in Rio de Janeiro, so pack your bikini and dancing shoes.

March

- Beach - experience the underwater world with a diving trip to Bali.
- Gastronomy - head to Australia for numerous food & wine festivals.
- Culture - a perfect time to explore Bombay coast and culture.

April

- Beach - relax and pamper yourself in a spa in Grenada.
- Culture - celebratwe the first day of summer in Iceland. It's something of a spectacle with street parties and colourful parades.
- City - head to Los Angeles, shop on Rodeo Drive, star spot in Hollywood and lap up the style of Beverley Hills.

May

- Beach - go island-hopping in the Greek islands, and enjoy a bit of culture in Athens or Crete.
- Culture - escape to Mexico for its fascinating Mayan ruins, vibrant culture and food, and fabulous beaches.
- Nature - it's cooler in Tanzania, a good time for safari - combine with a stint on a beach in Mozambique.

June

- Beach - up the glamour stakes on the beaches of St Tropez and Cannes.
- Spa - have an early summer in Florence, and stay at a luxury spa.
- City - wander through the souks of Marrakech for sunshine, culture and wonderful shopping.

July

- Beach - head to the South Pacific for some serious relaxation. Fiji, the Cook Islands and Tahiti have their dry seasons from May to November.
- Culture - cross North America in the trans-Canadian rail from Toronto to Vancouver.
- City - make the most of summer in Dublin, take in the sights and enjoy a cool pint of Guinness.

August

- Beach - soak up the sun on Italy's Amalfi coast.
- City - head to Edinburgh for the incredible international festival and stay at a boutique hotel
- Nature - explore the Lake District, walk the fells and drink afternoon tea.

September

- Beach - treat yourself to some luxury on the island paradise of Mauritius.
- Culture - temperatures are appealing this time of year in Sri Lanka. Laze on beaches, and cool off in the hill-top town of Kandy.
- City - enjoy late summer in Paris and head to Champagne in time to see the grapes being picked.

October

- Beach - jet off to the Seychelles for secluded luxury on a lush, tropical island.
- Culture - temperatures have dropped in Egypt, perfect for exploring the Pyramids, Luxor and Valley of the Kings.
- City - head to the east coast of the USA to experience the stunning colours of Boston and New England in autumn.

November

- Beach - savour the islands of St Kitts and Nevis in the Caribbean.
- Culture - Thailand is rich in culture with its markets, palaces and scenery. Soak it up before spending time enjoying the beach.
- Beach - year-round sunshine, excellent shopping and delux hotels make Oman a great honeymoon destination.

December

- Beach - spend Christmas in the lap of luxury on Turks and Caicos, where the temperatures are blissful.
- Culture - for a festive break, head to Lapland, where you can visit Father Christmas, ride on snowmobiles or go dog-sledding.
- City - savour the wine and sights of Vienna. Admire the Christmas markets and decorations, and spend a night at the opera.

Competition

WIN!
Halo Antibes King-size Bed

Beautifully Real Living from Halo

Halo travel the globe to bring you unique and beautiful living, dining and bedroom furniture. For over 30 years we have been producing furniture that's not only aesthetically beautiful, but practical too.

Our collections are inspired by the places we visit, from the treasures of India, to the beautiful leather of Italy and with craftsmanship originating from traditional English techniques.

Visit www.haloliving.co.uk to find out more about Halo and where you can see and purchase our beautiful furniture.

Whilst you browse for inspirational honeymoons from Luxury Backpackers, we would like to offer you the chance to win a beautiful brand new Halo Antibes king-size Bed (worth £699 at RRP), so you can continue to sleep well, even after your honeymoon!

To enter the prize draw, simply log onto
www.haloliving.co.uk/honeymoonsinstyle

halo
Est. 1976 haloliving.co.uk

Closing date 31st December 2009 see website for full terms and conditions.

eboutique

Itineraries: inspire your escape

To help you plan your trip or just help you with some inspiration... Luxury Backpackers offer a 'planning & booking' service from a flat fee of £50. We don't charge any commission and we are 100% impartial....passing on the best advice and best price directly to you. We offer a bespoke service and we can plan anything from a weekend escape to a gap year backpacking. Email us on info@luxurybackpackers.com

Guidebooks: planning your escape

Buy our first published guidebook **'Global Adventures in Style'** highlighting the best adventures and featuring 8 different destinations - Costa Rica, Belize, New Zealand, China, Thailand, USA, Italy and Mexico. Buy online via our eboutique, amazon.co.uk or from any good bookshop.

Visit **www.luxurybackpacker.com/eboutique**

BUY NOW

Canvas Prints: escapism in your home

A selection of our finest travel photography mounted on canvas and stretched on superior timber frames. Styles vary from travel ambience, people & places and scenery, depending upon your personal style and taste. Every photo has been exclusively shot by LBP (so no-one can copy your style!) each canvas also features a short story of where, when and how they were taken. Prices range from £40 to £160.

Imperial Palace in Tokyo. Taken in 2006. The current Imperial Palace (Kokyo) is located on the former site of Edo Castle, a large park area surrounded by moats and massive stone walls in the center of Tokyo. It is the residence of Japan's Imperial Family.

All sizes available

Seaplane in Fiji. Taken in 2004 in the Mamanuca islands, a plane landing to drop off some travellers. Travelling by sea plane is the most exhilarating and convenient way to travel around the 300-island archipelago of Fiji.

18 x 18 inch only

Sunset in Fiji. Taken on a still summer night in Fijian islands of the Mamanucas.

18 x 18 inch only

Beetle Taxi. Taken in Mexico City, 2005. Known locally as 'Vocho' it is considered the workhorse for the Mexican taxi industry, it never gives up!

18 x 18 inch only

Acknowledgments

A project such as this is a major team effort and relies on the help and generosity of many fantastic people all over the world. Jill & Carlo would like to sincerely thank:

Kerry Dennison, Pauline Dennison, Nicola Osmond-Evans, Sam Anson, Stephanie Tomkinson, Jane Anderson, James Meadows, Komodo Media and all the support from their friends and family.

Adventure Index

ISBN 978-0-9557397-1-2
Published by Luxury Backpackers Ltd 2008 in the UK

Luxury Backpackers Ltd Reg. No. 5661479
Address for Luxury Backpackers can be found on www.luxurybackpackers.com

Luxury Backpackers, Adventures in Style and the Luxury Backpackers Logo are trademarks of Luxury Backpackers Ltd and are registered in the UK Patent & Trademark Office. Luxury Backpackers Ltd makes every effort to ensure that all our books and company stationery are made from 100% recycled paper sources from post-consumer waste.

Printed in the UK

Designer: Stephanie Tomkinson